PAKISTAN AND AFGHANISTAN
THE (IN)STABILITY FACTOR IN INDIA'S NEIGHBOURHOOD

Edited by
KINGSHUK CHATTERJEE

Institute of
Foreign Policy Studies
(IFPS)

Centre for Pakistan
and West Asian Studies
(CPWAS)

Calcutta University
Kolkata

in association with

KW Publishers Pvt Ltd
New Delhi

First Reprint June 2013

The Court of Directors of the East India Company sent a despatch in July, 1854 to the Governor-General of India in Council, suggesting the establishment of the Universities of Calcutta, Madras and Bombay. In pursuance of that despatch, the University of Calcutta was founded on January 24, 1857. The University adopted in the first instance, the pattern of the University of London and gradually introduced modifications in its constitution.

The Institute of Foreign Policy Studies (IFPS) at the University of Calcutta is an autonomous centre devised for the study of international relations, with particular emphasis on foreign policy. Funded by the Ministry of External Affairs (MEA), Government of India, the institute purports to create a pool of foreign policy specialists capable of offering advice on matters pertaining to India's international relations. The Institute has already been earmarked for developing regional expertise with reference to the Government of India's Look East Policy, and that towards West Asia. The IFPS has also been chosen as one of the ten centres for United Nations Academic Initiative, functioning as the hub for studies on peace and conflict resolution.

The Centre for Pakistan and West Asian Studies, Calcutta University, was set up in 2005 under the UGC Area Studies Programme. It is the only research outfit associated with a University in eastern India with an exclusive focus on Pakistan and West Asian countries, Afghanistan, Iran and Iraq in particular, which together constitute a part of India's extended neighbourhood in the West. The Centre, since its establishment in 2005, has tried to develop a greater understanding of this extended neighbourhood by looking at the internal dynamics of the region with far greater detail than is generally accorded by other area studies outfits in the country.

© 2013, Institute of Foreign Policy Studies (IFPS) and Centre for Pakistan and West Asian Studies (CPWAS).

All rights reserved. No part of this publication may be reproduced, stored in a retrieval system, or transmitted in any form or by any means, electronic, mechanical, photocopying, recording or otherwise, without the prior written permission of the copyright owner.

The views expressed in this book are those of the contributors and do not represent the views of the Institute of Foreign Policy Studies (IFPS) and Centre for Pakistan and West Asian Studies (CPWAS).

ISBN   978-93-81904-62-6

Published in India by

KW
KNOWLEDGE WORLD

Kalpana Shukla
KW Publishers Pvt Ltd
4676/21, First Floor, Ansari Road, Daryaganj, New Delhi 110002
Phone: +91.11.23263498/43528107
Email: knowledgeworld@vsnl.net • www.kwpub.com

Printed and Bound in India

Contents

	List of Contributors	v
1.	Introduction	1
2.	Theorising the War on Terror: The Limits of Realism *Shibasish Chatterjee and Shreya Maitra Roychoudhury*	9
3.	Pakistan and Afghanistan: Of Instability and Umbilical Ties *Kingshuk Chatterjee*	35
4.	Dragon Splashing the Muddy Water: China in South Asian Region *Binoda kumar Mishra*	57
5.	India's Afghan Policy: America's Victory to Pakistan's Quagmire *Pramit Palchaudhuri*	73
6.	Urban Vulnerabilities in 'post-conflict' Afghanistan *Arpita Basu Roy*	89
7.	Pashtunwali and its Impact on Insurgency and Reconciliation Efforts in Afghanistan *Anwesha Ghosh*	111

8. Economic Impact of Terrorism:
   Case of South Asia Post 9/11   131
   Anindya Sengupta and Anshuman Tiwari

9. Cinematic Interpretations of Terrorism-Images,
   Identity and Impressions In Hindi Cinema   163
   Swati Bakshi

LIST OF CONTRIBUTORS

Swati Bakshi is a freelance journalist.

Arpita Basu Roy is a Fellow at Maulana Abul Kalam Azad Institute of Asian Studies, Calcutta.

Shibasish Chatterjee is Professor and Head, Department of International Relations, Jadavpur University, Calcutta.

Kingshuk Chatterjee is Assistant Professor, Department of history, Calcutta University.

Anwesha Ghosh is a Fellow at Maulana Abul Kalam Azad Institute of Asian Studies, Calcutta.

Shreya Maitra Roychoudhury is a UGC-JRF scholar at the Department of International Relations, Jadavpur University, Calcutta.

Binoda Kumar Mishra is Director, Centre for Studies in International Relations and Development.

Pramit Palchaudhuri is Foreign Affairs Editor, *The Hindustan Times*.

Anindya Sengupta is a member of the India Information Service.

Anshuman Tiwari is the Chief of National bureau, *Dainik Jagaran*.

1. Introduction

India's neighbourhood to the west, Pakistan and Afghanistan, can easily rank as one of the most volatile regions on the globe. Witnessing prolonged violence and instability for a little over three decades—ranging from two full scale foreign invasions and occupations to a civil war—Afghanistan virtually began to be seen by the international community as the epicentre of volatility in South and Central Asia, threatening to spill over its frontiers in almost all directions. In the course of the first decade of the 21st century, although many western observers began to argue that the epicentre was located on either side of the Durand Line, Pakistan was in as much danger of beginning to unravel as Afghanistan was, and the volatility in the region was much greater than it was previously suspected.

Observers and strategists based in India found some curious satisfaction in this I-told-you-so moment. India has long subscribed to the position that all volatility and instability in the region was squarely the responsibility of the trajectory of Pakistan's development since 1947, and what the Indian intelligentsia saw as a virtually inevitable slide towards Islamic radicalisation harvested in and exported from Pakistan. The consternation caused by the actual display of Islamic radicalism in action in Taliban-ruled Afghanistan, followed by the murderous militancy of Islamists inside Pakistan, seemed to reinforce the worst auguries put forward by Indian scholars about the subversive nature of Pakistan.

Given India's experience of Pakistan's waging of proxy war first in Khalistan and then Kashmir fomenting fissiparous tendencies, it was perhaps not an altogether unreasonable appraisal of the issue.

However, such essentialist understanding of the problem(s) cannot withstand the serious and hard questioning quite frequently put forward by specialists working on the region. Essentialism does not explain, for instance, why realism—considered a very important explanatory paradigm in the study of international relations—should stop at the frontiers of Pakistan and Afghanistan. Why would it appear to be more important for Islamabad that the regime in Kabul is Islamist than one which preserves order and stability after a period of foreign occupation and civil war? Or is it? Was the situation in Afghanistan wrecked by the 'tribal' character of the state? If so, would establishment of order necessitate 'detribalisation' of the state? How is that to be accomplished, if at all?

Even more significantly, the voices that emanate from the unstable neighbourhood itself also indicate a far more complex scenario than any essentialist reading would seem to put forward. If Islamist propensity is essential to the Pakistani psyche, why does it not afflict all the people of Pakistan? Does the appeal of Islamic radicalism run along tribal fault lines, and if so, why does it do so? If tribalism is intrinsic to Afghan society, could the international attempts at managing the situation be successful at all? Or would it require necessarily solutions that come up from the ground, rather than those imposed on the region from outside, by people who are not sensitive to the manner in which Afghanistan has evolved?

India cannot afford to neglect the matter of volatility in its neighbourhood, not simply because it involves its bête noire, Pakistan, but also because any long drawn conflict in the region could destabilise the larger neighbourhood in a way that would make its reverberations felt even in India. Indeed, India has been a victim of Pakistan's export of Islamic terrorism, and has been involved from quite an early date in trying to stabilise Afghanistan. Nevertheless, most of India's responses have often tended to be reactive, responding to situations that have already evolved rather than helping then to evolve. If a more durable solution has to be sought for the region, it requires to be continually assessed whether the region warrants greater and more sustained intervention. And for that, it is crucial for subtle and nuanced questions of the sort indicated above to be raised in a bid to understand the complexity of the situation that makes India's neighbourhood to the west as volatile and unstable as it actually is.

The Institute of Foreign Policy Studies, Calcutta University, has set itself the task of promoting better understanding of the contexts in which foreign policy is formulated, and means to feed into the academic and bureaucratic discourse that evolves on India's foreign policy. The Centre for Pakistan and West Asian Studies, by contrast, is essentially an Area Studies unit, meant to work towards the same objective as that of the IFPS. The present volume comes for all practical purposes out of a seminar held by the IFPS in collaboration with CPWAS at Calcutta University in March 2012. The volume comprises of eight essays, highlighting on various approaches to the question of instability in India's western neighbourhood, and what it could mean for India.

In the first paper, Shibasish Chatterjee and Shreya Maitra Roychoudhury examine the relevance of realism as an analytical paradigm to understand the War on Terror, which has heavily conditioned the trajectory of Pakistan and Afghanistan in the last decade. The paper argues that while realism can offer a cover for military intervention, it provides no explanation for the root conflict as yet. Against realism, 'securitisation' can be pitched as a superior theoretical explanation of the ensuing conflict in Afghanistan that now also involves Pakistan directly. Chatterjee and Maitra Roychoudhury argue that the conventional theoretical formulation of realism is inadequate in analysing multiple political entities operating at both international and sub-national levels. They recommend overcoming this inadequacy by introducing the dynamics of securitisation instead.

They argue that the conflict needs be viewed primarily through the lenses of identity and security rather than the standard canons of realism.

Kingshuk Chatterjee's paper tries to attempt just such a synthesis, although not entirely following the theoretical model recommended in the first essay. Looking at the Pakistani entanglement in Afghanistan as a question not of identity heavily conditioned by the realist tools of analysis, the paper purports to raise a few questions about the nature and reason behind Pakistan's involvement in Afghanistan. Unlike most other commentaries on the matter, the paper aims to plot Pakistan's involvement in Afghanistan not merely as a factor of its strategic vision and foreign policy, but also to explore the extent these were occasioned by the dynamics of Pakistan's domestic situation. The paper means to cast doubt on the hope that the Afghanistan problem could be resolved simply by throwing more resources into the region, leaving untouched some of the core structural problems that have come to characterise it.

Binoda Kumar Mishra's essay is essentially from a hard realist position, looking at the extent to which Chinese involvement in Afghanistan and particularly its proximity to Pakistan has heavily vitiated the security landscape in the subcontinent. Mishra argues that Chinese diplomatic and material support for Islamabad is one of the principal factors encouraging Pakistani adventurism in China. He accounts for such risky behaviour on Chinese part not in terms of any attempt to cock the snook at India, rather in an endeavour to boost its own well-defined national interests of keeping India hemmed in. Mishra however goes on to argue, the strategic rationale has of late been supplemented by Chinese hunger for resources, which has taken it into Afghanistan, climbing on to the back of Pakistan. Most interestingly, he concludes that China might eventually have to rethink its policy lest the rise force of political Islam produces undesired outcomes in Xinjiang—something that might compel Beijing to help address the matter of instability in the neighbourhood.

Pramit Palchaudhuri's essay is meant to give a sense of the thinking in the Indian establishment on the question of Afghanistan. He contends that as Afghanistan was becoming Pakistan's quagmire, India gained a degree of leverage it had not had since 9/11. He moots the point that India has increasingly come to exploit the situation in Afghanistan to push forward its agenda regarding Pakistan. India, he suggests, has had a policy that has been 'AfPak' from the very beginning. Palchaudhuri identifies three distinct phases to India's policy to Afghanistan after the fall of the Taliban regime in 2002. The first was defined by what was an effective military partnership with the US designed to overthrow the Taliban regime, reduce Pakistani influence in Afghanistan and undermine the use of Afghanistan as a base for terrorist activity against India. The second phase ran between 2008 and 2010 defined by Indian fears of a US military withdrawal from Afghanistan and the degree it would affect the security gains that New Delhi had harvested with the fall of the Taliban regime. The last phase resulted from the collapse of US-Pakistani strategic ties following the assassination of Al Qaeda leader and terrorist, Osama bin Laden, inside Pakistan. India came to accept that a US withdrawal would not be as sweeping as originally thought, that a Taliban takeover of Kabul was not imminent and the costs this would impose on Pakistan could be useful to India's own policies regarding Pakistan.

Arpita Basu Roy's essay deals with the manner in which Afghanistan's urban transition is precipitating a crisis in local governance. Against an analysis of peace-building and post-conflict reconstruction, the paper argues that Afghanistan's urban poor has little or no access to basic services and social infrastructure because of a result of limited resources, combined with the authorities' unwillingness and lack of capacity to serve effectively. It analyses situation in the different urban spaces in Afghanistan and shows that there are determinants that shape and differentiate the situations of the poor and the vulnerable. By interpreting the various vulnerabilities as human security threats, it shows how exclusion from basic services adversely affects the capacity of the urban poor to earn adequate income and acquire the necessary human assets to have quality of life. By highlighting the crises of urbanisation, the paper argues for democratic representation and efficient urban management.

The erection of a democratic apparatus in a semi-modern polity atop a traditional society, however, is not exactly a cakewalk. Structures of traditional society frequently impede the process of such an endeavour. Anwesha Ghosh's essay concerns itself with one of the mores of traditional society that might actually strengthen a modern democratic polity in Afghanistan. The paper aims to bring back into the discourse the factor of *Pashtunwali*—a system of values and rules of behaviour, which for a rather long time before (and after) the rise of Taliban has been an integral feature of the Pashtun way-of-life. The paper means to explore its significance in the present-day. Even today, it has arguably a substantial hold among the Pashtun majority provinces of Afghanistan and tribal areas on the Pakistani side of the Durand Line. The paper finally chooses to examine if it can play a role in the Afghan insurgency, as also the reconciliation efforts in contemporary Afghanistan.

The paper by Anindya Sengupta and Anshuman Tiwari takes an unusual approach to the issue of instability in subcontinent. They present a preliminary analysis of the damage caused by terrorism, a phenomenon that has become almost a part of the security scenario of the subcontinent. They examine the extent to which the South Asian experience could be analysed through methodology established in the West in a bid to understand the long run and more invisible costs extracted by uncertainty and insecurity both in the realms of economy, and secondarily also in issues pertaining to restrictions in the public space. The paper confines itself to study mostly the direct economic consequences of terrorism, and the extent to which changes are brought about in economic behaviour in a local or regional setting.

The final essay does not deal directly with the question of instability in India's neighbourhood. Swati Bakshi's essay deals instead with the impact on the Indian *mentalite* of this ever-increasing ambience of insecurity, through the case study of one particular matter in one particular medium—representation of Muslims as the unwitting 'other' in mainstream Bollywood films. Approaching the question from the stand point of culture of representation, Bakshi argues that the principal change in representation of the Muslims as an almost unconscious equation with Pakistani, Afghan or secessionist enemies of the Indian 'self'. Bakshi indicates that this depiction was largely at variance with the initial depiction of Muslims in Indian film as integral to the nation-building project. She marks 9/11 and the arrival of the War on terror in the Indian subcontinent as crucial milestones in this process.

2. THEORISING THE WAR ON TERROR: THE LIMITS OF REALISM

Shibasish Chatterjee and Shreya Maitra Roychoudhury

Realism and the War on Terror

Why did the US and the West wage 'war on terror' in Afghanistan? Was their military action based on power calculations? This paper examines the relevance of realism, among conventional international relations theories, in seeking answers to these questions and explaining the conflict. The paper argues that while realism can offer a cover for military intervention, it provides no explanation for the root conflict. Against realism, 'securitisation' can be pitched as a superior theoretical explanation of the ensuing conflict in Afghanistan that now also involves Pakistan directly. It is, therefore, critical that we admit the theoretical limits of realism and pursue the dynamics of securitisation in this case. This paper submits that the conflict be viewed primarily through the lenses of identity rather than the standard canons of realism.

Realist theories explain state behaviour by power and/or security considerations within an anarchical environment either by invoking meta-psychological cognates or structural variables. The realist ontology is overwhelmingly pervaded by the state and fundamentally static. The only change it countenances is over the distribution of power. The realist view of world politics is configured in terms of inter-state rivalries. Realists are however divided over the modalities of power calculations and the relation between power and security. Most forms of realism, therefore, do not offer sociological explanations of conflicts. We need to elaborate this a little more.

Although realism remains the most powerful paradigm in International Relations, it does not represent an undifferentiated and consistent body of thought. Realism, despite its popularity in conventional International Relations scholarship, has become a much-divided approach. This is not the place to engage in debates with realism. However, before moving to the controversy between defensive and offensive varieties of realism, certain basic or core premises of the approach will be identified. To begin with, the realists of all shades are primarily concerned with the question of war and peace in the international system, their causes and conditions, variations and possibilities of transition from one condition to another. Despite the difference between classical realism and structural realism, with the former being more unit-oriented (state-based) and the latter distinctively structural, all forms of realism take the structure of the international relations as a necessary condition to explain various trends in world politics. Both classical and structural varieties of realism believe in the idea of structural anarchy, although their definitions and formulations of this notion vary. Realism remains committed to the idea of security dilemma, according to which, the international system being a self-help system is perpetually unstable and risky, for the search for security of one becomes the cause of insecurity for its adversaries.[1]

Realists are divided over the critical issue of how much power a state requires for its security, a point to which we would return later. In fact, this is the central point of contention between defensive realists and their offensive counterparts, with the former operating with a status quo bias and the latter being completely revisionist. However, all forms of realism are essentially focused on the question of relative capabilities of states in an environment bereft of a central regulatory mechanism. Thus for realists, unlike many other ideologies, conflict is a natural condition of the international order, a rather axiomatic state of affairs than as a consequence that can be attributed to larger, macro-sociological or politico-economic factors. Another premise that joins all realists is their focus on territorial units, states, as the central actors of world politics. Despite globalisation and manifest weakening of the capabilities of the state in different parts of the world, realists remain committed to the state as the dominant actor of world politics. The idea of a rational, unitary state remains, therefore, a central element of realism. The final premise that characterises nearly all forms of realism is that states are claimed to be guided by the considerations of national interest, usually defined along survival, security, material development, and enhancement of relative capabilities. The concept of national interest supposedly provides realism with a 'rational hypothesis' and aids in overcoming the fallacies of concern with beliefs, motives, ideologies and preferences of decision-makers.[2] All such premises are analytically indefensible.[3] Despite such blatant fallacies, realism dominates the IR discourses at least partly because of its parsimony, its innate simplicity based on common sense or prudence, and its accessibility to policy makers across time and space.

It has been more than a decade since the US invaded Afghanistan during the first administration of President Bush following the terrorist attacks of September 2011. The key reasons for the US war in Afghanistan remain Al- Qaeda, the threat of a sanctuary and base for international terrorism, and the fact the conflict now involves Pakistan's future stability. Till now, the US has reportedly deployed one hundred thousand troops and allocated about US$ 300 billion in Afghan war efforts. At present, the United Nations Security Council-backed and NATO-led International Security Assistance Force (ISAF) comprises of 1,30,000 soldiers of which 90,000 are American. Despite this, the inability of the allies to secure success in the war has been explained by realism as the prevalence of singular focus on national interest of each partner rather than any concerted security concern of all. British Prime Minister David Cameron's stated strategy seemed a case in point when in March this year, he defined 'doing the job in Afghanistan' as leaving the country, looking after its own security, not being a haven for terror without the involvement of foreign troops.[4] Moreover, without qualifying as official actors as states within the realist paradigm, poorly equipped guerrilla groups, Al-Qaeda and Taliban have proven to have the military capability and personnel to keep a major power—the US—from succeeding. Military commanders in Afghanistan describe the Taliban as composed of three tiers; a hardcore of ideologically committed militants, a second layer of 'fellow travellers' pursuing agenda that overlap with those of the Taliban such as feuds or drug trafficking, and a third tier of foot soldiers fighting for a mixture of reasons.

Obama administration refocused its energy in order to 'disrupt, dismantle and defeat Al-Qaeda in Pakistan and Afghanistan, and prevent their return to either country in the future'[5]. The US fights this crucial war mostly because it fears terrorist attacks from Afghanistan; as President Obama said, "It is from here that we were attacked on 9/11, and it is from here that new attacks are being plotted as I speak."[6] The US must continue to wage war as it cannot let Afghanistan turn into a safe haven for Al-Qaeda to coordinate terrorist attacks. An article published in December 2010 by the Center for a New American Security further demonstrates these US security interests:

> "The United States has a vital interest in preventing AQAM (Al-Qaeda and associated movements), groups committed to violent and even catastrophic attacks on American citizens and soil, from returning to safe havens in Afghanistan akin to those they enjoyed prior to the terrorist attacks of September 11, 2001. The United States also has a vital interest in continuing to degrade and disrupt AQAM and eliminate safe havens in Pakistan in order to prevent future attacks against the United States and its allies."[7]

Recently, the US piloted a proposal to 'separate' the Taliban from Al-Qaeda since it now holds that the Al-Qaeda and the Taliban belong to two 'different fields of action'; unlike the Al-Qaeda which is a global organisation, the Taliban is 'Afghanistan-centric'. It sought to remove twenty Taliban figures from the United Nation's (UN's) list and pushed for a range of changes to the UN's so-called '1275 list', which comprises around 450 terrorists belonging to Al-Qaeda and Taliban.

Realism helps to explain aspects of foreign policy that remain consistent over time. From a realist perspective, governments (or 'states') go to war either motivated by the considerations of power or security being situated in an international system in which each state faces threat from other states as there is no central regulatory authority like domestic government. Classical realists and neo-classical realists argue that national leaders rationally calculate costs and benefits of military engagement in terms of their state's power and security. States' international behaviour, thus, is a matter of both structure and agency, for all states are constrained by the international system structure though the degree of restraint varies according to the relative capacity of states. In this regard, the shift from a bipolar distribution of power during the Cold War to unipolar US military dominance caused US strategy to guard against the policies of and balance against threatening 'rogue' states. Unipolar dominance after the Soviet Union's collapse has lowered the appeal of security through multilateralism and collective security, and increased reliance on unilateral strategies based on own is military strength.

Whether the current configuration of forces makes unilateralism or multilateralism the more preferred strategy divides realists. Walt argues that 'the UN and other international institutions help the US exercise its power in a way that is less threatening (and therefore more acceptable) to others'.[8] Michael Mastanduno explicitly derives from Walt's balance of threat theory the proposition that 'the dominant state in a unipolar setting will rely on multilateralism in its international undertakings'.[9] Randall Schweller and David Priess agree, noting that 'if the hegemon adopts a benevolent strategy and creates a negotiated order based on legitimate influence and management, lesser states will bandwagon with rather than balance against it'.[10] Scholars like Brooks and Wohlforth, in contrast, explain why unilateralism is the stronger urge for the US and argue, "The problem is that there is no counterbalancing against the United States, nor is there likely to be any time soon. Indeed, the remarkable thing about the current international system is that three key causal factors highlighted by realist balance-of-power theory itself are configured so as to make the reemergence of traditional balancing dynamics among the major powers highly improbable."[11] The three factors they cite are (1) geography, (2) the distribution of material capabilities, and (3) the accomplished fact of American hegemony in contrast to a revisionist aspiration. These make unilateralism attractive for the US. In their words again, "Taken individually, each of these factors militates against counterbalancing. Together they make it exceedingly unlikely, for there is considerable positive interaction among them. American preponderance in the material scales of world power feeds the collective action and coordination problems, as do geography and the status quo barrier."[12]

Realism's emphasis on continuity and on the inevitability of military competition and war among sovereign states gains credence from the fact that, despite changes in leadership and despite the collapse of its main rival, the US did not diminish its military spending after the end of the Cold war. Rather, the Clinton administration pursued an arms buildup so that US militarily outspent any combination of potential rivals and, in addition, bombed Serbia without the UN authorisation. The Bush administration has been forthright about its goal of global hegemony—a power so complete that challenging it becomes nearly inconceivable. Bush's (2002) West Point speech declared, "America has, and intends to keep, military strengths beyond challenge." Given this strategic objective, overthrowing Saddam Hussein's government can be understood as an effort to enhance US reputational and symbolic power beyond challenge—particularly after the September 11, 2001 attacks that might have made the US appear vulnerable.[13]

Realism asserts that for the US, the dual threats of Al-Qaeda-inspired terrorism and nuclear proliferation into terrorist hands are vital issues of national interests because they threaten the state and its citizenry directly and thus legitimise the war on terror and complementary emergency legislations.[14] Striving to remain committed to the goal of absolute victory in Afghanistan, President Obama has increased the number of American troops in Afghanistan by another 30,000 in 2010. The US and its allies are engaged in the war against Al-Qaeda not only in Afghanistan but also inside Pakistani borders, which makes Pakistan a pivotal actor in this war. Since 2007, Afghanistan itself has urged the coalition on the 'war on terror' to track down the 'strongholds of Al-Qaeda and Taliban which are 'outside Afghanistan', or in other words, in Pakistan. The US intelligence officials have maintained that though there is no formal assessment, it is accepted knowledge that Pakistan's tribal areas along the border with Afghanistan have become an accepted haven for al Qaeda leaders such as Osama bin Laden and Ayman al-Zawahiri.[15] In 2008, following US-led air strike against Taliban in restive tribal areas of Pakistan, bordering Afghanistan President Hamid Karzai issued the first open threat to send troops inside Pakistan by stating that his strife-torn country has the right to dismantle terrorist nests in the neighbouring country in self-defence.[16] Senior American military and intelligence officials have repeatedly stated that Taliban leaders, showing surprising levels of sophistication and organisation are using their sanctuary in Pakistan to stoke a widening campaign of violence in northern and western Afghanistan. The uncovering of Osama bin Laden's hideout in Abbottabad and his killing last year vindicates the assumption. Unfortunately, the cross-national, wide network of Al-Qaeda outposts also dilates the war on terror beyond the territorial restrictions of the Afghan borders. As international law complicates waging an all-out war inside Pakistan, the US cannot stem Pakistan's involvement from places like Waziristan. The political conditions in Pakistan, thus, become of utmost significance for the US and have substantial consequences for national security. The CNAS report in 2010 also claimed that the stability of Pakistan concerns the US as its vital interest. It states:

> "The United States cannot allow Pakistan's nuclear weapons to fall into the hands of violent extremist organizations or any other enemy of the United States. Accordingly, the United States supports a strong Pakistani state capable of maintaining control of both its nuclear arsenal and its territory, particularly from internal threats. The outcome of events in neighbouring Afghanistan will play a key role in the ultimate stability of the Pakistani state. A return to Afghan civil war could embolden Pakistan's own internal insurgency, potentially undermining Pakistan's fragile stability."[17]

Even though Pakistan is a major recipient of US aid and is expected to jeopardise its own internal security with the spawning of Al-Qaeda and Taliban elements, it has shown insignificant action in combating the terrorists on its soil. For example, though Presidents Karzai and Musharraf agreed in 2007 to fight terrorism, deny sanctuary, training and financing to terrorists in each other's countries, Pakistan has been accused of being behind numerous killings in Afghanistan, including the attempt to assassinate President Karzai in 2008. The Obama administration had to particularly renew its efforts to get the Pakistan government to be more aggressive about the killing or capturing of Taliban leaders inside Pakistan. However,

Pakistan's military leadership resents that contrary to earlier pledges, the US has bypassed the Inter-Services Intelligence and the Central Intelligence Agency operatives have begun networking directly with various militant organisations. For example, through two months of sustained grilling of the US' ace intelligence operative Raymond Davis in a Lahore jail by the ISI, the Pakistani military leadership learnt about the CIA's penetration of Pakistan's body polity.

Pakistan's evasive behaviour on the issue may be understood as yet another manifestation of the realist goals of power and security. Given India's apparent dominance in South Asian politics and the historical legacy of amity-enmity with Pakistan, Afghanistan provides a unique opportunity to the latter to maximise its security interests. Afghanistan has always acted as a buffer between Pakistan's territory and other nations in the neighbourhood. With the foundation of Bangladesh, its strategic significance was enhanced. Thus, Pakistan is systematically strategising to maintain and increase its power and security in the region by keeping Afghanistan within its sphere of influence, and trying to articulate a regime in Kabul that is controllable by Islamabad. Pakistan's major concern is its rival neighbour, India, not Al-Qaeda; in fact, Pakistan is a reluctant fighter, as it has no real concern for the Al-Qaeda. As Robert D. Blackwill puts it, "The Pakistani military, driven by its perception of India's the enemy and its perceived requirement for strategic depth, will not end its support for and provision of its sanctuary to its longtime Afghan Taliban proxies or accept a truly independent Afghanistan."[18] Although historically the rivalry between India and Pakistan is rooted in their dispute over Kashmir, the tense Indo-Pak relationship is mostly due to continuous security competition and the struggle to increase their relative powers in the region. One view holds that Pakistan-India security competition through interfering in Afghanistan has turned this war into almost a defeat for the US and NATO nations. Pakistan has used billions of US aid, which it received to fight terrorism, on developing and modernising its military capacities against India and gain 'strategic depth' in the region. In fact, Pakistan has abused the US aid to balance against India while leaving Al-Qaeda to gain strength inside its borders. Thus, Pakistan's military competition with India has hampered the US progress in defeating Al-Qaeda. Pakistan seems to be ostensibly promoting an undemocratic regime in Afghanistan by destabilising and blocking any progress towards a stable and self-reliant Afghan government. In 2010, Pakistan offered to play a central role in resolving the Afghan war and mediating with Taliban factions, in order to stem the 'growing Indian presence there'.[19]

A careful observation of the developments reveals that India is also seeking to increase its political hold in Afghanistan at the cost of Pakistan's influence. Although India, unlike Pakistan, does not share common borders with Afghanistan, it has been trying to create friendly relations with Afghanistan since 2001. Afghanistan, after Bhutan, is the second biggest recipient of aid from India. Additionally, India is the fifth biggest donor of aid to Afghanistan on the global scale. The current volume of assistance stands at US$ 700 million. In May 2011 alone, fresh aid worth US$ 500 million was pledged. Interestingly, Indian aid to Kabul has served security interests like buying warlords, deepening political clout, pressurising Pakistan, and gain steady access to Central Asia. Clearly, Afghanistan has become the ground for the inter-play of India-Pakistan's aspirations for regional dominance. Addressing the Afghan Parliament and implicitly referring to Pakistan's anticipated designs, Prime Minister Manmohan Singh stated, "Afghanistan is integral to our security and both of us are aware of this. Our ties are as old as time. Our cultural and religious links are unshakeable. And our Afghan brothers are aware of this and know our commitment to stand by in readiness should anyone be thinking in terms of security vacuum occurring after the NATO forces withdraw from the region."[20] Rahimullah Yusufzai, a well-known BBC reporter for the Khyber region has stated that India and Pakistan are fighting a 'proxy war' in Afghanistan. At an international conference held at Camden in 2010, Teresita Schaffer, the Director of South Asian Program at the Center for Strategic and International Studies in Washington D.C., confirmed America's acknowledgment of Indo-Pak rivalry in Afghanistan. Pakistan's major objective in Afghanistan, she says, is 'to minimize India's influence-down to zero—if at all possible', and in response, India wants 'that Pakistan be the only game in town'.[21] Perhaps, it is very difficult for the US to reach victory in the war in Afghanistan if it has to meddle between two rival nuclear nations, Pakistan and India.

Strategists have observed in the past that war between India and Pakistan, two nuclear-armed nations, or the spread of destabilising Islamist insurgencies to the states of Central Asia would be disastrous. Further, state failure in Pakistan—owing to financial crisis, popular unrest, or insurgent disruption—could upend the region's fragile balance of power in potentially catastrophic ways. A Taliban return to control in Afghanistan would energise the global jihadist movement, motivate insurgent groups in Pakistan and across the region, endanger democracy and human rights in Afghanistan, and deal a blow to widely held standards of freedom and justice in the region and around the world. An Afghan civil war fought by proxies of regional neighbours could also prove a destabilising and bloody outcome of a precipitate US departure.

Under the circumstances, realists acknowledge that there are grave difficulties and severe limits to what the US can strategically achieve in the war against terror in the AfPak region. Clearly, the current military strategy in Afghanistan is not working in its current form. Robert Blackwill says, "The United States and its allies are not on course to defeating the Taliban militarily... Nor with an occupying army largely ignorant of local history, tribal structures, languages, customs, politics and values, will the Alliance win over large numbers of Afghan Pashtuns, as counter-insurgency doctrine demands."[22]

During the very early stages of the conflict, many hundreds of thousands of Taliban and Al-Qaeda personnel were killed in a carefully coordinated covert war involving US, British and Australian special forces and operatives on the ground with northern-alliance fighters. Combined, these men directed the US air power onto specified targets and within weeks, the Taliban regime crumbled. Many realists advocate that by using unmanned and armed drone reconnaissance planes, satellites and stealth-bombers, a well-conducted and persistent air-war against Al-Qaeda targets directed by small special-forces groups and internal Afghan forces would severely disrupt the ability of Al-Qaeda to operate freely within the country. Combining this strategy with the retention of a force in Afghanistan to train up a new Afghan army seems a real and plausible alternative to the current stalemate. However, realists also realise that reliance on force alone may not bring success. As Fotini Christia and Micahel Semple observed, "The overriding lesson of the US experience in Iraq—first its failures and most recently its successes—is that no occupying power can hope to quash an insurgency by killing and capturing its way to victory. It must make friends, especially among its enemies. In Afghanistan, a counter-insurgency strategy that includes a credible attempt at reconciliation is more likely to achieve stability that one that relies solely on foreign troops and victories in the battlefield."[23] Victory by engineering defection in the ranks of the Afghan Taliban who wish to remain by the winning side, or a strategy of guarded reconciliation, one that builds on the distinction between the good and the bad Taliban, is also a possible realist strategy. Nevertheless, unless the US led coalition forces understand what makes the Taliban, even this defter and subtler version of the realist game plan would not work.

Before moving on to the real deficiency of realism as a theoretical guide to the War on Terror in Afghanistan, a couple of more points need some attention. First, the US came to invade Afghanistan to destroy the terror apparatus of Al-Qaida networks. Its grouse against the Taliban was the former's support of the Al-Qaida networks, particularly for providing safe haven to Osama Bin-Laden. In keeping with the realist understanding of terrorism, it targeted the state that sponsored such networks. While it ousted the Taliban regime swiftly, it failed to destroy the Taliban movement. The Taliban is not merely a government or a regime; it is also a revanchist and deeply conservative social movement. While realism can weld a strategy against enemy states or regimes, it has nothing to offer against adversarial social movements. Hence, despite the presence of foreign troops and superior firepower, the Taliban could quickly regroup again. Moreover, a statist counter-insurgency strategy, premised upon and modeled on state conflict, cannot succeed against terror networks that require fighting terrorism as a transnational network, by multinational cooperation and police coordination. Realism's preference for high politics, the use of the armed forces, and its statist ontology, make it very difficult to wield a counter-insurgency strategy against forces that are more attuned to low politics remain structurally fluid and networked, and are not entirely comprehensible in statist terms.

Secondly, many experts believe that a realist strategy that relies only on force will not work here. The US Secretary of Defence, Robert Gates, submitted before the Senate Armed Services Committee in January 2009, "If we set ourselves the objective of creating some sort of Central Asian Valhalla over there, we will lose because nobody in the world has that kind of time, patience and money." As Paul D. Miller recognised, "US policy makers and the public increasingly doubt that the war can be won."[24] The argument here is that unless the Afghan state is revitalised, democratic institutions created and strengthened, ethnic peace brokered under multilateral supervision, stakeholders turned into responsible agents committed to constitutional limits, the economy kick-started and growth maintained, and safety ensured through local means, no long lasting peace will be possible in Afghanistan. The realists err by over-emphasising the military aspect of the problem; they have little understanding of the corresponding need to invest into institution building and governance so that the use of force can yield positive benefits in the long run. As Miller pointed out, "The Taliban were able to regroup and launch an insurgency because, effectively, nothing stood in their way. The Afghan government was still unable to offer services or resolve disputes, and there were too few international soldiers to rescue the country. The state's institutional capacity remained weak, the rule of law was nonexistent, and the security services were still embryonic."[25] While realism theoretically has no quarrel with strong institutions and governance, it has very little explanation of how these may become an integral part of a counter-insurgency strategy.

What Realism Cannot Account for: Identity and Social Construction
The centralised military authority in Afghanistan had been able to underpin internal peace until 1973 when the palace coup that brought Sardar Daud to power shattered the equilibrium. Since then, ethnic tensions and divisions have deepened, problematising the maintenance of internal order. American and NATO forces began phased withdrawal from Afghanistan starting summer of 2011 and announced total disengagement by 2014. But the unpreparedness of the Afghan forces to assume complete charge of the security scenario persuaded the modification in their stance, resulting in the NATO forces remaining keeping control over some 'heavily contested areas' and maintaining residual presence in an advisory capacity even beyond 2014. Much has been done to train and equip

the Afghan military and police to revive the military command, but it seems a tall order. In this situation, the task of improving regional governance and security will increasingly fall upon Afghanistan's neighboors and near neighbours—Iran, Pakistan, India, China, Russia, and the Central Asian States. These regional actors had been engaged in the Afghan war (and its spillover effects—civil war, cross border terrorism and civil strife) since the late 1970s. Pakistan has been, and for the foreseeable future is likely to be a key player in the region. Pakistan's involvement in Afghanistan has led to transformative political, economic, and social consequences at home, breeding religious militancy, and escalation in suicide attacks disrupting societal peace and harmony, and deepening the crisis of governance. Over three million Afghan refugees moved into Pakistan and changed the demographic composition and culture of many parts of Pakistan—heroin trade, drug addiction, proliferation of portable arms and cross border terrorism emerged as serious new governance challenges. Consequently, over these decades a complex web of jihad, sectarianism, and extremist groups became a potent force, changing the complexion of Pakistani State and society.

Any meaningful engagement with the dynamics of the conflict in Afghanistan and a search for ways to quell the ongoing cycle of violence will inescapably have to grapple with the ethnic question.[26] The conflict is essentially about securitising identities along ethnic and religious lines. It is not about any universal quest for power involuntarily experienced by certain nation-states. Both the Afghan and Pakistani cases bear testimony to this. Identity is a function of the 'nation' (as opposed to the state) and the societal sector. Securitisation theory argues that state and societal boundaries are rarely coterminous. State and society of even the same people are two different things; while the state is based on fixed territory and formal membership, societal integration is a more varied phenomenon, possibly occurring at both smaller and larger scales and sometimes completely transcending territorial scales. Societal insecurity and the need for securitisation of identity occurs when communities of whatever kind define a development or potentiality as a threat to their survival as a community. Societal security, on the other hand, prevails when these large, self-sustaining 'we' identity groups are able to win over another/other self-defined identity groups. Migration, horizontal competition, vertical competition, and depopulation are the possible issues, which pose threats to identity communities and by that logic, to societal security. The choice of whether to see societal threats as a task for society itself, as one for an existing state, or as an argument for gaining or regaining statehood can have a decisive impact on regional dynamics.[27]

Thus far, much of the discourse at the popular level and to a considerable extent even within the academia and policy circles has tended to categorise Afghan society into more or less neat, fixated, and territorialised ethnic categories. Categorisation of such nature not only goes against the operational reality of these categories on the ground but it has also led to the formulation of disturbingly un-informed policy propositions at the highest level. Instructive in this regard are certain proposals to sort out the Afghan quagmire, forcefully put forth by a distinguished former US diplomat, Robert D Blackwill. Using the platform of the influential US think tank *Council for Foreign Relations* Blackwill has formulated a case for partitioning Afghanistan along ethnic lines:

> "De facto partition of Afghanistan is the best policy option available to the United States and its allies... We would devote nation-building efforts to the north and west region where, unlike the Pashtun, people are not conflicted about accepting US help... Washington should not wait to change its objective and strategy in Afghanistan until even more US blood and treasure have been lost in a fruitless quest among the Afghan Pashtun."[28]

Partition as a solution to endemic violence and conflict is based on realist prescriptions from scholars like Van Evera and Barry Posen that seems thoroughly misplaced in this case. Blackwills partition argument in fact appears to be subtly premised on a degree of ethnic stereotyping which ascribes a certain fundamentalist pre-disposition as inherent among the Pushtuns. Furthermore, the argument is based on the empirically flawed belief that ethnic groups are more or less neat, geographically bound frozen cultural units. The futility of such an analysis is powerfully underscored on two counts: first, the social-cultural history of the region now known as Afghanistan does not affirm categorisations of such a nature. Second, recent trends in the ongoing conflict in Afghanistan point to a spread not just of the Taliban insurgency itself into what were considered the impregnable areas of Northern Afghanistan—populated largely though not exclusively by ethnic minorities comprising Tajiks, Uzbeks and Turkmens—but a steady rise in the recruitment of non-Pashtuns in Taliban ranks.[29]

Furthermore, while interventions on this thematic do to an extent engage with certain factors that shaped the trajectory and politics of the identity discourse at the regional and local levels in the country, however, they do so in a limited sense by confining their frame of reference to state actors at the regional level and elites at local level. They overlook in particular the role of certain other key players—trans-national criminal networks, which often have an interest in keeping conflicts alive and the role of lonely and anxious diaspora communities. Finally, no realist has sought to engage with the significant role played by two factors—first, none have attempted to examine the role played by religious networks of *madrasehs* and sufi orders who posses strong religious, moral and social capital and are thus potentially poised to play the role of both spoiler as well as peacemaker, and second, the role played by history and memory in shaping the image of the 'other', especially significant in pre-dominantly non-literate societies like those of Afghanistan where oral tradition retains a seminal role, has gone completely unaddressed.[30]

The attempt is to pursue the argument that the conflict in Afghanistan has not been per se an ethnic conflict arising from 'ancient hatreds' and/ or irreconcilable clash of ethnic differences. Instead discrimination and deprivation (both perceived and real) determined by ethnic differences created a receptive niche for what Edward Azar famously referred to as 'Protracted Social Conflict' (PSC). The resulting 'disarticulation between the state and identity groups' constitutes the core of such conflicts. The trajectory of conflict is shaped in decisive measure by the crucial role of state in satisfying or frustrating a group's identity needs.[31]

Securitising identities is also responsible for the present predicament in Pakistan, overlaid in this case by strong geo-political interests. Pakistan is peculiarly complex in terms of its ethnic and linguistic compositions. Each of its provinces is associated with a single ethno-linguistic group: Punjab with Punjabis, Sindh with Sindhis, Baluchistan with Baluchs, and the Northwestern Frontier Province (NWFP) with the Pashtuns.[32] It has always been replete with ethnic imbalance and the sense of difference was exacerbated with Jinnah's highly centralised political system and the increasing predominance of the Mohajirs and the Punjabis in the colonial-styled administrative structure. When ethnic discontent initially spurted out, the state resorted to methods of cultural imperialism with its centralising and homogenising tendencies. Urdu was imposed as the national language even though it commanded only 3.7 per cent of the population. Bengali and Sindhi languages were replaced by Urdu as the medium of instruction.

The partition of Pakistan in 1971 seriously affected its identity as a state, and witnessed a shift of power from the secular mainstream forces towards aggressive Islamists. The conservative Islamists of the Northwest Frontier province and Baluchistan were significantly empowered. Zulfikar Ali Bhutto prepared the stage by banning alcohol in army messes, introducing moral instructions in officer training schools, pursuing bilateralism in foreign policy with emphasis on special ties with the Islamic world, and proclaiming a vision of Pakistan as an Islamic and socialist state. However, it was General Zia ul Haq, who consciously securitised religion in Pakistan by declaring that Pakistan should be guided by Islamic principles and that Islam (or any other religion, if it was deeply held) made man a better citizen or professional. He tried to foster Islamic ideology in Pakistan, going so far as to declare that the 'preservation of that Ideology (Pakistan ideology) and the Islamic character of the country were as important as the security of the country's geographical boundaries'.[33] Jinnah was reinterpreted as an Islamist and not a secular politician during Zia's regime and the Ulema was elevated to the role of the vanguard, though they had played a marginal role in the creation of Pakistan. The cultural divide in Pakistan deepened, and sharply ran along north-south through the country, transcending provinces, becoming conspicuous in the more cosmopolitan cities of Lahore, Karachi, and Faisalabad. The internal threat from virulent Islamisation was pampered with American support during this time for Zia in Pakistan as well as the mujahidin in the anti-communist Afghan jihad.

In the post 1971 period, despite the experience of a second partition, Pakistan's political leadership remained intolerant and authoritarian to ethnic expressions. Bhutto dismissed the nationalist assertions of the Baluchistan government and fanned extremist, underground, guerrilla war with the armed forces. However, the political leadership consciously attempted to move away from a South Asian cultural orientation of multi-ethnicity and embraced Middle Eastern, specifically Saudi Arabian, religious identification and connection. This served a dual purpose: legitimacy for the army that had lost its credibility after the defeat of 1971 and ensuring the rise of Saudi religious influence in Pakistan. In this case, domestic imperatives and a new geopolitical identity came together. Gradually, Pakistan became a fierce ground of contested identities as the influence of Wahhabi Islam with its vicious anti- Shiite and anti-Sufi beliefs increased significantly in Pakistan, particularly in the tribal areas bordering Afghanistan. As the geopolitical worth of Pakistan increased dramatically with the Soviet invasion of Afghanistan in 1979, this began to impact upon the societal basis of its identity, particularly over the role of Islam as the defining ideology of the nation. This identity contestation in Pakistan spilled over in its relations across frontiers, both vis-a-vis India and Afghanistan, and had profound consequences for the region as a whole. By the mid-1990s, Pakistan had a degree of independence from foreign support and its influence extended over Afghanistan and Central Asia as part of a strategic imperative and a 'civilising mission'. Pakistan's Afghan adventure was attractive to Saudi Arabia. The geopolitical stakes of the Pakistani establishment in Afghanistan and the appeal of religious extremism began to reinforce and sustain each other.

As Pakistan became increasingly schizoid, its relations with India assumed greater complexity. Buzan *et al* assume that the conflict between India and Pakistan has an intrinsic societal element as the root cause stems from the inherent incompatibility of principles linking politics and identity in the two countries. India not just straddles a variegated ethnic complexion but is also multi-confessional, perhaps posing to Pakistan, the insecurity of subsuming the entire continent. Pakistan, on the other hand, is religiously based and through this particularist logic, questions the secular federal basis of India. Simultaneously, the intra-societal conflicts within India and Pakistan have created dynamics of insecurity, which provoke defenders of the state and its identity project against a variety of ethno religious entities willing to challenge the state on the grounds of being unable to maintain their identity within it. Vertical identity conflicts between the states and the societal entities within them assume shape, and this necessarily exacerbates resorting to coercive strategies and military means by the two countries against each other. Pakistan has tensions among its Punjabis, Pathans, Baluchs, and Sindhis, and its main port—Karachi—is plagued by ethnically-based political and criminal violence. India has a variety of ethno religious secessionist movements, most conspicuously the Sikhs and the Kashmiris.[34] Tensions between its Hindu majority and Muslim minority continue to generate regular outburst of communal violence, and the rise of Hindu nationalism as a political force could threaten the founding basis of the Indian state, thus forming a new insecurity scenario for India and Pakistan in South Asia.

While instigating and abetting terrorism in different parts of India had become a convenient strategy for Pakistan, as the conflict over Pakistan's identity became more accentuated, terrorism assumed new dimensions. Terror emerged as an inevitable accompaniment of that contestation, as the state was besieged by identity questions that threatened its very foundation in a crucial way. For, Islam as a defining identity of the Pakistani nation became contested from within, a challenge that is categorically different from the one coming from rival bases of identity like language or ethnicity. As Islam was securitised, the concomitant role expectations following from it also became divergent. For the Wahhabis, terrorism was no mere strategy in Pakistan's protracted Manichean struggle against India; rather, it seemed a violent but existentially inescapable manifestation of a certain idea of selfhood, premised on a particular understanding of religiosity, which liberated terror from a specific geographical reference. In other words, terrorism ceased to be justified as violence of the weak against the injustice of the strong in Kashmir; it became rather an aspect of societal identity that is purely self-authenticating and self-legislating in character. Pakistan's new geographies of fear and terror are thus bereft of territorial anchors. They are intimately connected to debates and contestations over Pakistan's identity where religion itself has been securitised by a plethora of actors.

As Pakistan is increasingly drawn into a crisis of meaning, its engagement in South Asia has come to mirror its predicament. The foundation of the state based on faith has made it impossible for the political elite to shift the terms of debate over its self-hood. As new actors pose the role of religion differently compared to its past, the state is left with no other option but to reinforce the securitisation of its identity residing in faith. In other words, Pakistan will find it impossible to normalise its ties with either India or Afghanistan unless it politically decides its own self. While selves are many so is politics born out of them. The identity that will dominate the political narrative of Pakistan will decide the trajectory of its external engagements in South Asia.

Conclusion

The US- and NATO-orchestrated war on terror has till now been executed in a manner that lends credence to the core realist assumptions, identifying the relevant, geo-strategically involved states as the major actors and their respective struggle for securing national interest and power as instrumental in shaping the matrix of conflict. The increasing strength and prevalence of non-state actors like the Taliban and Al-Qaeda and the ethics of jihad have also been conceded through the lens of state backing and support. However, with the growing consensus that the military tactics and haphazard counter-insurgency measures of the US and NATO forces are failing to bring about the desired results of stability in Afghanistan and the eradication of extremism, it becomes necessary to urgently acknowledge the theoretical limits of realism in providing an apt conceptualisation of the conflict. A redesigning of the war on terror hinging on a deeper, contextualised understanding of the ongoing dynamics becomes imperative. The sociological understanding of conflict rendered possible by the securitisation approach offers valuable theoretical tools in building a more comprehensive account of the inter-play of local dynamics in Afghanistan, Pakistan, and India in offsetting the war on terror. It is also instructive in seeking avenues to thoroughly resolve the crises and bridge the real and perceived gap between the willingness of the state machinery and demands of the innumerable identity groups. Engaging in the securitisation discourse subsumes possibilities for refining the analysis of the multi-faceted and multi-layered interactions between the US, Afghanistan, Pakistan and India and finding a new steering course for the war on terror. Calculating the socio-political dimensions of sectarian violence and ethno-nationalism in Pakistan is bound to gain considerable emphasis in this discourse, as it has clearly become the fulcrum of the conflict.

It is important to recognise that therapeutics like weeding out terrorism or fighting extremism will therefore not work beyond a point. Unless faith as a basis of self-hood is de-securitised, Pakistan's domestic contestations over identity will continue to shape its relations with the outside world. Experts disagree sharply about Pakistan's instability and vulnerability in the face of a US and ISAF defeat in Afghanistan. There is no way to predict how well Pakistan can secure its border and deal with its own Islamic extremists, and Pakistan is both a nuclear state and a far more serious potential source of support to other extremist movements than Afghanistan. A hard-line Deobandi-dominated Pakistan would be a serious strategic threat to the US and its friends and allies, and would sharply increase the risk of another major Indo-Pakistani conflict. But outside intervention cannot any longer be economically sustained and though may be sanctioned by realism will make little difference in this case. And even if realism continues to shape Western/US thinking, the utter superficiality of it will not contribute to any better or more substantive understanding of this immensely complex social and political drama now unfolding in Pakistan. The future of what remains of the War on Terror does no longer depend on what others 'do' but hinges critically on how Pakistan resolves itself, more specifically in its politics of violent securitisation of selfhood.

Notes
1. See Kenneth Waltz, *Theory of International Politics*, (New York: McGraw Hill, 1979).
2. See Hans J Morgenthau, *Politics Among Nations: The Struggle for Power and Peace*, (New York, NY: Alfred A. Knopf., 1948).
3. John A. Vasquez, *The Power of Power Politics: From Classical Realism to Neotraditionalism*, (Cambridge, MA: Cambridge University Press, 1998).
4. *The Economist*, March 17, 2012, p. 23.
5. BBC News, "Obama Diary- Day 61-70; Friday March 27, 2009". http://news.bbc.co.uk/2/hi/americas/7959878.stm (Accessed on May 28, 2012).
6. The White House. Speeches and Remarks, Remarks by the President in Address to the Nation on the "Way Forward in Afghanistan and Pakistan", December 01, 2009. http://www.whitehouse.gov/the-press-office/remarks-president-address-nation-way-forward-afghanistan-and-pakistan (Accessed on May 28, 2012).
7. David Barno and Andrew Exum, "Responsible Transition: Securing US Interest in Afghanistan Beyond 2011", Centre for a New American Security, December 2010, pp. 9-10. http://www.cnas.org/files/documents/publications/CNAS_ResponsibleTransition_BarnoExum_2.pdf
8. Stephen Walt, 'Keeping the world "off balance": Self-restraint in US foreign policy', in G. J. Ikenberry, ed. *America unrivaled: The future of the balance of power*, (Ithaca: Cornell University Press, 2002, p. 143).
9. Michael Mastanduno, 'Preserving the unipolar moment: Realist theories and US grand strategy after the cold war', in Ethan B. Kapstein and Michael M. Mastanduno, (eds.), *Unipolar politics: Realism and state strategies after the cold war*, (New York: Columbia University Press, 1999), p. 147.
10. Randall L. Schweller, and David Priess, "A tale of two realisms: Expanding the institutions debate", *Mershon International Studies Review*, vol. 4, no. 1, 1997, p. 24.
11. Stephen G. Brooks and William C. Wohlforth, "International Relations Theory and the Case against Unilateralism", *Perspectives on Politics*, vol. 3, no.

3, September 2005, p. 511.
12. Ibid. p. 512.
13. *New York Times*, Text of Bush's Speech at West Point, June 01, 2002. http://www.nytimes.com/2002/06/01/international/02PTEX-WEB.html?pagewanted=all (Accessed on May 28, 2012).
14. Sikandar Ahmadi, "The War in Afghanistan", Aamozgar, July 2011. http://www.aamozgar.org/the-war-in-afghanistan
15. CNN World, Analysts: "Al Qaeda has safe haven in Pakistan frontier", January 24, 2007. http://articles.cnn.com/2007-01-24/world/pakistan.qaeda_1_al-qaeda-al-zawahiri-pakistani-authorities?_s=PM:WORLD (Accessed on May 29, 2012).
16. "Karzai warns Islamabad over terrorist nests" *The Hindu*, June 16, 2008, p. 14.
17. Barno and Exum, op. cit. 9.
18. Robert D. Blackwill, "Plan B in Afghanistan: Why a De Facto Partition is the Least Bad Option", *Foreign Affairs*, vol. 90, no. 1, January/February, 2011, p. 43.
19. "Pak Seeks US deal to Keep India Out", *The Asian Age*, February 11, 2010, p. 1.
20. "The Long Road to Kabul", *The Statesman*, May 20, 2011, p. 7.
21. Teresita Schaffer, "Afghanistan and Pakistan in Turmoil—The View from India; India's growing role as a world power". Camden Conference on Afghanistan, Pakistan, India-Crossroads of Conflict, Camden 2010. http://www.camdenconference.org/2010-conference/2010-conference-highlights/# (Accessed on May 29, 2012).
22. Blackwill, op. cit. p. 42.
23. Fotini Christia and Micahel Semple, "Flipping the Taliban: How to Win in Afghanistan", Foreign *Affairs*, vol. 88, no. 4, July/August, 2009, p. 35.
24. Paul D. Miller, "Finish the Job: How the War in Afghanistan Can Be Won", *Foreign Affairs*, vol. 90, no. 1, January/February 2011, p. 51.
25. Ibid. 59.
26. Raghav Sharma, "Managing Identities in Fragile States: The Case of Afghanistan". http://www.brandtschool.de/fileadmin/downloads/About_us_PDFs/Veranstaltungen/CSMP/Research_Abstract_Sharma.pdf?PHPSESSID=52ec209eab7be7cdc9d655bdbf003c1e (Accessed on May 26, 2012).
27. Barry Buzan, Ole Waever and Jaap de Wilde, Security: *A New Framework of Analysis*, (London: Lynne Rienner, 1998), pp. 119-122.
28. Robert D. Blackwill, "A de-facto Partition for Afghanistan", *Council on Foreign Relations*, July 07, 2010. Accessed at http://www.cfr.org/publication/22920/de_facto_partition_for_afghanistan.html (Accessed on May 26, 2012).
29. Sharma, op. cit. 3-4.
30. Ibid.

31. Edward E Azar, "The Management of Protracted Social Conflict: Theory and Cases", *Dartmouth Publishing Company.* April 1990.
32. Stephen Philip Cohen, *The Idea of Pakistan,* (Washington: The Brookings Institution, 2004), p. 201.
33. Ibid. 84; also Cohen et al, *The Future of Pakistan,* (Washington: The Brookings Institution, 2011), pp. 1-2.
34. Buzan et al, op. cit, pp. 133-134.

3. PAKISTAN AND AFGHANISTAN: OF INSTABILITY AND UMBILICAL TIES

Kingshuk Chatterjee

Introduction

In March 2009, within two months of his entry into the White House, Barack Obama established the hyphenated term 'Af-Pak' as central to the discourse on the US policy in the region. Believed to have been coined by Richard Holbrooke in February 2008,[1] before Obama lent it the weight of White House's official usage, the term has excited much disapproval in Pakistan, where people have resented being hyphenated with their much devastated and 'backward' neighbour—a resentment which has been voiced by many, right from President Asif Ali Zardari, who observed: "Afghanistan and Pakistan are distinctly different countries, and should not be lumped together in the generic label of AfPak."[2] Regardless of whether one endorses the usage of the term AfPak, Obama's original contention that the situation in Afghanistan cannot stabilise without greater involvement in Pakistan warrants serious consideration – even though not simply for the reason he advanced.[3] That the trajectory of two countries is intertwined, is a belief that even some of the Afghans have aired in public. The Afghan President Hamid Karzai is on record referring to Pakistan as a 'twin brother'.[4]

While it is necessary to listen to what politicians and statesmen have to say, it is equally important not to take them literally. It is, thus, important to acknowledge that at present, the imbroglio in Afghanistan has repercussions in and for Pakistan, and vice versa; it is also essential to figure out whether the two are inextricably intertwined, and if not then how did the trajectories of the two become so entangled that the problems of the one cannot be resolved without the good offices of the other.

This paper does not presume to look into the extent of Pakistani involvement in Afghanistan over the last few decades. It merely purports to raise a few questions about the nature of and reason behind such involvement. Unlike most other commentaries on the matter, the paper aims to plot Pakistan's involvement in Afghanistan not merely as a factor of its strategic vision and foreign policy, but also to show how these were occasioned by the dynamics of Pakistan's domestic situation. The paper further means to raise the question whether the international community is living in a fool's paradise by believing that the Afghanistan problem could be resolved simply by throwing more money and resources into the region, leaving untouched some of the core structural problems that have come to characterise it.

Pakhtunistan as a factor in Pak-Afghan Relations
Created in 1947 combining the Muslim majority provinces of British India, and partitioning the largest two of these, Punjab and Bengal, Pakistan's territory was originally divided into two parts—East and West Pakistan—with India wedged in between. Because of the persistent friction between New Delhi and Islamabad that resulted in three wars and an abiding sense of suspicion, mistrust and acrimony, in many ways the two countries have taken to define each of their 'selves' in the mirror image of the 'other'. The visualisation of Pakistan as the territorial space for the Muslims of the Indian subcontinent may have successfully held its own against the Congress vision of (Composite/Hindu) India, it failed to address issues of linguistic and ethnic diversity that existed inside Pakistan. The transformation of East Pakistan into the sovereign state of Bangladesh in 1971 indicated the finality of Islamabad's failure in that respect. Admittedly, the challenge of ethnic diversity to the

process of state-formation in Pakistan has been relatively much weaker; nevertheless one of the issues that plagued Islamabad from the very beginning was the irredentist claims of Afghanistan on the Pakhtun-dominated regions east of the Durand Line.

The Durand line lays down the 2,560 km long boundary that Pakistan shares with Afghanistan. Finalised in 1893, its principal objective had been to establish the British in areas they considered strategically significant to safeguard the Empire in the subcontinent from any prospective Russian penetration, in the event that the buffer kingdom of Afghanistan failed to stop it. Although Kabul was in no position to resist Mortimer Durand, (the designated representative of the Raj) depending as it did on British India to hold the Russian bear at bay, the then Emir of Afghanistan, Abdur Rahman, registered his protest at the manner in which he was being deprived of his legitimate over-lordship of all Pushtu-speaking people, or Pathans/Pashtun/Pakhtun, a substantial segment of whom were to now lie east of the proposed Durand Line.[5]

The significance of Emir Abdur Rahman's protest becomes clear when it is put in perspective. The modern kingdom of Afghanistan was cobbled together in course of the 17th century (in the wake of the disintegration of the Persian-speaking empires of the Safavids to the west and the Mughals to the east) by a Pushtu-speaking tribal confederation under the leadership of the Abdali clan, also known as the Durranis. The kingdom gradually came to be styled as Afghanistan, that is, 'land of the Afghans' (a term which by this time was being used interchangeably with Pashtun or Pathan)—so called because the principal holders of authority were Pakhtun by origin. Nevertheless, the territory brought under the Durrani banner had historically been one of the crucial overland trade routes connecting South and East Asia with the Middle East and Central Asia—thus, people of other ethnic backgrounds, such as Turkics (Tajik, Uzbeg, Turkoman) and Mongols had settled down across the ages in the region, principally towards the northern reaches of the country adjacent to Central Asia. It is difficult to pronounce authoritatively in this matter in absence of any definite demographic records, but it would seem that the proportion of Pashtun-speakers in the kingdom tended to be somewhere between 50 and 60 per cent of the total population. The Durand line changed this favourable ethnic balance significantly against the Pakhtuns, reducing their proportion to somewhere between 40 and 45 per cent of the total population.

When the state of Pakistan came into being in 1947, Kabul as much as New Delhi believed that the fledgling state was not very likely to survive on account of its multiple ethnicity and geographical peculiarity of the newly-formed state of Pakistan.[6] Kabul contended that all treaty arrangements with the Raj were at an end, and sought the return of the Pakhtun-dominated areas that the British had acquired first by the treaty of Gandamak (1879) and then imposition of the Durand Line—both of which Kabul claimed to have accepted only under duress. A rather weak argument, given that Kabul had affirmed the finality of the Durand line in subsequent agreements in 1905, 1919, 1921, and 1930.[7] Mindful of the weakness of its case from the standpoint of international law, Kabul then resorted to calling for a referendum for the Pakhtuns of the northwestern part of Pakistan to vote on whether they would choose to secede and constitute a separate state of their own called Pakhtunistan. Kabul even became the only country to vote against Islamabad's entry into the UN till the frontier issue was resolved.[8] The idea presumably was if the Pathans of North-west Frontier Province (NWFP) voted to secede from Pakistan, it would not be able to stay independent for long and thus would be sucked into Afghanistan.[9]

During 1950-55, low-scale Afghan subversion into the tribal regions (in much the same manner that Pakistan was later to do in Kashmir) prompted Pakistan to proclaim its intention to consolidate its authority among the tribals of the Afghan frontier.

This occasioned a major diplomatic incident that resulted in the withdrawal of ambassadors by the two sides, and relations did not return to normal before 1957.[10] In 1960-61, Pakistan and Afghanistan actually got entangled into such an intense clash over the Khyber border that they completely severed all diplomatic relations with each other. Eventually Tehran brokered a détente between Islamabad and Kabul in 1963 that held for ten years.

The Pakhtunistan concept resurfaced in 1973, upon the ouster of the King Zahir Shah by his cousin Muhammad Daoud Khan. Daoud in fact went a step further and argued that Pashtunistan should involve not merely the NWFP and FATA, but also the Baluchistan region, which has nearly as many Pashtuns as it has Baluch-speaking people.[11] The agenda of creating a Pashtunistan remained alive in the years that followed till the Soviet invasion, principally owing to Daoud's active fostering of the disaffection in both NWFP and Balochistan, posing a very strong irredentist threat that Pakistan could not afford to ignore.

Repercussions of Pakhtunistan on Pakistan
The potency of the Pakhtunistan threat for Pakistan cannot be exaggerated. At the time of its birth, Pakistan was confronted with the need of creating a new economic space for itself, losing as it did its historic economic catchment area that India provided. Since the agricultural production of the two most populous provinces, Punjab and Bengal, used to cater to the demand from of the Indian subcontinent, the dislocation thus caused in the economy of the regions that became Pakistan was considerable. Coming atop the human dislocation of the partition, affecting more than 17 millions on either side of the border, 1947 scarred the nascent country badly. The attempts to come to terms with the experience of partition and the need to create a country anew resulted in the generation of a series of structural dynamics that were virtually *sui generis* in

the subcontinent, and have influenced the subsequent trajectory of Pakistan as a country largely.

In 1951, four years after it came into being, the total population of Pakistan was approximately 76 million, of which West Pakistan was 33.8 million, while the more populous East Pakistan was a little over 42 million. The population of West Pakistan nearly doubled in 1972, standing at 65.32 million, but the loss of East Pakistan meant the population stood at merely half of what it used to be. Moreover, the loss of East Pakistan implied the loss of more than half of the territory that Pakistan had at the time of its creation – and this was, understandably, a national trauma. But even more significantly, 1971 marked the beginning of a second major attempt to create a self-contained economic entity with, almost literally half the human, territorial and material resources for Islamabad. The vista of a fresh territorial loss by way of a separate Pakhtunistan was still less acceptable in 1971 than it might have been in 1947, not least because of the psychological blow this would have delivered—one can safely say, Pakistan would have disintegrated had it materialised. This was not simply because of the psychological blow, however. The demand for Pakhtunistan that began to surface in 1973 involved not merely approximately 10 per cent of the land that NWFP constituted (74,521 sq km), but also Baluchistan, which constituted more than half of the entire landmass of Pakistan (3,47,100 sq km out of the total national area of 7,96,096 sq km).[12]

Needless to say, the Pakhtunistan problem was not simply the outcome of Kabul's instigation. The mainstay of the economy of the various provinces that constituted Pakistan happened to be agriculture, in the east as much as the west. In the first two decades after 1947, a major thrust was undertaken in developing a manufacturing sector, which went on to transform the economic character of much of Punjab and lower Sindh, particularly around Karachi. The demographic weight of Pathans and Balochs being merely 10 per cent of the population of West Pakistan, development by and large left the regions untouched. This led to major disaffection among both the Baloch and the Pathans. The successful breaking away of East Pakistan encouraged regionalist ambitions, especially among the Pathans of both NWFP and Balochistan. The Nationalist Awami Party (NAP) formed coalition governments in NWFP and Baluchistan alike campaigning on a strong regionalist agenda, and in particular advocating keeping of NWFP and Baloch provinces together, playing to the Pakhtun interests there.[13] The NAP coalition governments were dismissed eventually in 1973 by Zulfikar Ali Bhutto, largely because of its growing proximity with Kabul.[14]

As Pakistan began its crackdown on Pakhtun and Baluch nationalism, Kabul's support for such dissidents coupled with its denunciation of Islamabad's genocidal treatment of ethnic minorities in international forum. Islamabad saw this as 'the greatest threat to Pakistan's since the secession of East Pakistan'.[15] Bhutto's government responded with a two pronged policy. On the one hand, the Baluch and Pakhtun nationalist forces were cracked down upon; on the other, Islamabad began supporting violent Islamist factions in Afghanistan that resisted centralisation of political authority that Kabul was keen on.[16] It calculated that Islamist factions would emphasise more on the common confessional character of the Afghans, and play down the ethnic diversity; such a policy would undermine the notion of Pakhtunistan as well.[17]

The proximity Kabul enjoyed under Daoud with both Moscow and New Delhi was an additional incentive for Islamabad's involvement in Afghanistan. Moscow's support involved considerable latitude for the communist-inspired People's Democratic Party of Afghanistan (PDPA), who eventually got entangled into a power struggle with Daoud, leading to his deposition in April 1978. The dramatic attempts at centralisation and modernisation introduced by the PDPA invited such a backlash from the regions that the Soviets had to step in during the fateful summer of 1979. Once the US decided to thwart the Soviets in Afghanistan, Pakistan emerged as a willing associate by routing American funds to the Islamist resistance against Soviet occupation just as they had funded resistance to Daoud's centralisation. Islamist factions led by Burhanuddin Rabbani and Gulbuddin Hekmatyar were among the principal beneficiaries of Pakistani support both before and during Soviet occupation.[18]

The Afghan war turned out to be a double-edged sword for Pakistan. The country witnessed a cash infusion into the state because of the Afghan war to the tune of US$ 3.2 billion over a period of six years (1981-87), and then another US$ 4.02 billion after 1987.[19] There was the additional factor of a massive influx of over 3 million Afghan refugees, of whom all but 2,00,000 settled down in Khyber Pakhtunkhwa, FATA, and Baluchistan.[20] The situation was conducive to the rise of the Mujahideen, which saw the region becoming awash with arms. The spillover effect that occasioned as a consequence accentuated internal migration away from the frontier regions. This in turn caused sectarian conflicts in Sind, ethnic conflicts in Baluchistan, and most importantly the Islamisation of the politics of Punjab.[21] Together, these constitute the four greatest challenges before Pakistan today.

The Afghan Misadventure and the Internal Dynamics of Pakistan
The resonances of the Afghan misadventure of Islamabad needs be put in perspective. For a country that began as an essentially agricultural economy, and then managed only moderate level of industrial activity, Pakistan's urban population has increased more than five times over since 1951. Between 1980 and early 1994, a period when Islamabad posted smallest figures by way of economic growth, the growth in urban population averaged 4.6 per cent per annum. By early 1994, about 32 per cent of all Pakistanis lived in urban areas. While urbanisation progressed fastest in Punjab and

Sind,[22] it affected the trajectory of the other provinces also: the slowest rate was to be seen in Khyber Pakhtunkhwa, where the urban population grew from 11.1 per cent to 16.9 per cent while that of Balochistan nearly doubled from 12.4 per cent to 23.9 per cent.[23] In Punjab and Sind, where much of this urban population growth was the result of high rates of natural population growth (births minus deaths) and the in-migration of people from villages looking for economic opportunities and better living conditions, as also the usual 'push factors' (landlessness, indebtedness, uneconomic holdings).[24] But probably the most notable phenomenon for the rising urban character of Pakistan is the process of 'in-place urbanisation', that is, increase of population density of a rural region high enough for it to warrant urban facilities and services (streets to be aligned and named, drains to be built, waste disposal system to be put in place) creating what are known as ruralopolises. Such ruralopolises have transformed the Peshawar valley of Khybar Pakhtunkhwa since 1979.[25]

The most momentous demographic transformation that has been unfolding in Pakistan in the last few decades is to be seen in the frontier regions of Baluchistan, FATA and Khyber Pakhtunkhwa. The huge influx of refugees from Afghanistan may not have disturbed the overall ethnic make-up of Khyber Pakhtunkhwa, but the linguistic preponderance of Pushtu over languages like Hindku are quite evident—Peshawar, traditionally a predominantly Hindku speaking town has been swamped with speakers of Pushtu. In Baluchistan, the transformation can be measured by the fact that Baluch is no longer the predominant language spoken in the provincial capital, Quetta—it has been replaced by Pushtu. Far more significantly, instead of the easygoing traditionalist practice of Islam that used to characterise both these regions, the western provinces of Pakistan are becoming known for their social conservatism and assertive Islam.[26]

The impact of the influx of Afghan refugees is felt most in material terms in the realm of the economy of the three frontier provinces of Khyber Pakhtunkhwa, FATA and Baluchistan. The population of Khyber Pakhtunkhwa increased from 11 million (1981) to over 17 million (1998), registering an increase of over 60 per cent; that of FATA increased from 2.1 million to 3.1 million for the same period, registering a rise of almost 25 per cent; the population of Balochistan rose from 45 million to over 65.7 million, an increase of almost 50 per cent.[27] The frontier-regions happen to have the weakest economies of the country with agriculture characterised by disguised unemployment, and little manufacturing that is capable of generating jobs beyond the mining sector. One of the side-effects of this pattern was that after having steady rates of annual growth in unemployment hovering at around 1.64 per cent all through the 1970s, by early 1980s it stood at around 3.6 per cent; by 1999-2000 unemployment rates had climbed up to 6 per cent, and reached a peak of 7.7 per cent, with the number of unemployed population standing at 3.6 million.[28] In 2004, Baluchistan recorded more than 17 per cent of its population being without a job for more than 10 years; the same figures for inhabitants of the province aged between 15 and 24 was almost 34 per cent, and for those between 25 and 34 stood at 11 per cent.[29] Age disaggregated figures are not available for FATA, but overall unemployment and underemployment rates stood at over 50 per cent in 2007.[30] This has to be posited against national unemployment rate in Pakistan which stands at 15.4 per cent (2010), with youth unemployment standing at nearly half of that figure.[31]

The incidence of illiteracy is quite high in Pakistan, standing at over 50 per cent, (37 per cent for men and 64 per cent for women), which limits the pace at which skill-oriented service sector could expand in the country. Within Pakistan, literacy rates vary from one province to the next. While literacy levels are higher in Punjab and Sind (at 59 per cent) over the national average, Khyber Pakhtunkhwa equals the national average (approximately 50 per cent) while Baluchistan is slightly lower (at 45 per cent). But in the Federally Administered Tribal Areas (FATA) the level is as low as 22 per cent. This literacy deficit did not really affect the economy of Pakistan significantly till right through the 1980s (when the deficit was actually even greater) because Pakistan exported not merely skilled labour (viz. doctors, engineers, technicians, educators, etc.) to the Gulf states, but also less skilled ones (viz. security personnel, as in countries like Saudi Arabia where Pakistanis make up the bulk of expatriate security contingent); it happened for a long time to be the only growth sector in Pakistan's economy. Beginning in the 1990s, however, people without the benefit of any specialised education, found the pace of expansion of economic opportunities in the Gulf slowing down considerably, and almost grounding to a halt after 2000. At the same time, with the rapid economic liberalisation undertaken in the late 1990s, the economic opportunities for less-skilled individuals in the more traditional sector of the economy also began to disappear.

Given the rapid transformation of the demographic and economic scenario in Pakistan, the dislocation caused in Pakistani society is quite palpable. Steady growth of population, increasing pressure on land, urbanisation, economic stagnation, and surging consumerism have all contributed in the widening of disparities between the rich and the poor in Pakistan.[32] The impact of all these factors is most deadening in FATA, where by an official estimate, more than 60 per cent of the people live below the poverty line in 2007; corresponding figures for Khyber Pakhtunkhwa has improved from about 40 per cent in 2004 to about 17 per cent in 2007.[33]

It is largely in this background of demographic and economic dislocation that the flourishing constituency of militant political Islam in Pakistan needs be contextualised. As the population grew by about 50 per cent, and the urban population by about 80 per cent in the 1960s, and then by another 30 per cent overall and 50 per cent in urban population by the 1970s, the demographic growth put tremendous strain on Pakistan's resources, especially on its provision of civic amenities. Activities of Islamic voluntary outfits in the difficult days of 1960s and 1970s in the realm of *tarbiyah* (education) and *tanzim* (organisation) helped create a space in the public sphere for Islamic organisations, spreading from largely urban areas to suburbs as well. The repeated failure of the state in these areas fuelled sustained disaffection against it. By the 1970s, the *madraseh* emerged as an alternative education system especially in the Khyber Pakhtunkhwa, FATA and Baluchistan, courtesy the efforts of such voluntary organisations, as also local initiatives to introduce affordable education where the state is negligent, especially in the countryside.[34] Estimates suggest that beginning from only 137 *madrasehs* in 1947, the number climbed up to 908 in 1971, and then 1,745 in 1979, churning out clerics who in turn went out to set up or join other *madraseh*.[35]

Zia's policy of Islamisation was meant as a sop to this growing disaffected mass, mediated by the Islamic groups such as the Jama'at-e Islami. Coming to power after the spectacular failure of the Bhutto era in addressing Pakistan's social and economic problems, Zia al-Haq era (1977-88) resorted to militarisation and Islamisation of the Pakistani state as a panacea for the problems plaguing it largely than ever before. Confronted with mounting social tensions all across the country, he resorted to policies with an overt Islamic intonation—juridical reforms (such as the introduction of Shari'ah courts), implementation of the Islamic Penal Code, encouragement of Islamic banking and a new educational policy. The reform of the entire juridical apparatus, along with the Hudood Ordinance of 1979, (sanctioning the implementation of an Islamic Penal Code by administering punishments recommended in the Qur'an and the Sunnah), magnified the space available for the social and political forces rallying behind the banner of Islam.[36]

All this, however, happened at a time when population grew by nearly 50 per cent and urban population by over 90 per cent (1981-98), thereby heightening dislocation in Pakistani society. Moreover, the end of the Afghan adventure had brought back the *jihadi* forces in Pakistani society.[37] The Pakistani state tried to redirect these militant elements towards Kashmir, resulting in a kind of uneasy calm. But the disquiet over retraction of state patronage, that Zia had accustomed the lower and lower-middle class Islamist constituency to, began to grow in the wake of the liberalisation programme of the 1990s. Grievances against the political class mounted as evidence of rampant corruption of both the principal parties (Pakistan People's Party and Pakistan Muslim League-Nawaz) were brought to light by each other as much as the media. In 1994, the Pakistani government was faced with an armed insurrection in the Malakand region of Khyber-Pakhtunkhwa, led by Tehrik-e Nifaz-e Shari'ah-e Muhammadi, demanding the institution of the Shari'ah, indicating erosion of faith in the political elite.[38]

The demand for Shari'ah has, however, an additional dimension. With the Islamisation of the Pakistani urban and suburban landscape under Zia, with the introduction of the Shari'ah courts on the one hand, and reduction of state ability to provide the educational requirements of all its subjects, the number of *madrasehs* have grown in Pakistan at a rapid pace. As against only 2,861 *madrasehs* in 1988, the number of *madrasehs* in operation in 1995 was 3,906, which nearly doubled by 2003 to reach the figure of 7,000 and going past 13,500 by 2006.[39] A regional breakup of the *madrasehs* show that of the 6,561 *madrasehs* in operation in 2000, the province of Punjab alone had around 3,153 *madrasehs,* more than double the figure for 1988 (1,320) and more than three times that for 1979, before the outbreak of the Afghan crisis. Khyber-Pakhtunkhwa, facing the brunt of Afghan refugee influx, saw the number of *madrasehs* jump from 218 (1979) through 678 (1988) to reach 1,281 (2000). Similarly, while the number of *madraseh* in Sind increased less than three times over (380 in 1979, to 905 in 2000), the very sparsely populated Baluchistan province saw corresponding figures jump from 135 (1979) to reach 692 (2000).[40] Bulk of the students of this educational system stand little chance of being absorbed in the mainstream of modern Pakistani economy, either as industrial workforce or as expatriate workers in the Gulf. Quite apart from the belief they may have in Islamic value systems and jurisprudence, the institution of the Shari'ah would provide them with not merely a way of preventing the rot of 'unIslamic' consumerism that characterises modern Pakistani social and political elite, but also greater opportunities of gaining a livelihood. Thus the inclination to sign up for an agenda to overturn the existing dispensation is great among the products of the *madraseh* network, accounting for the growing violence that seems to characterise Pakistani society today. Given the paucity of state-funded and/or western educational institutions in the three frontier regions, the social impact of such radicalisation is found to be the greatest in Baluchistan, FATA and Khyber Pakhtunkhwa. Indeed, not all the students educated in the *madraseh* system necessarily resort to violence. However, it is difficult to ignore that an overwhelming majority of acts of militancy in the name of Islam are carried out by groups educated in one *madraseh* or the other.

The Urge to Cut the Umbilical Cord
Given the dislocation caused by the demographic transformation of Pakistan's frontier regions, Islamabad has a far greater interest in the stability of its neighbour than any other country. However, given its predicament, Islamabad needs not merely a stable regime in Afghanistan, but actually one that is committed to, and able to pave the grounds for, the precipitate return of Afghan refugees. Failing that, it would at the very least want a regime in Kabul that would not want to destabilise Pakistan with the spectre of Pakhtunistan. Hence,

after the Soviet pull-out Islamabad began to support the Pakhtun warlord Hekmatyar, hoping he would be able to inspire the refugees to return home. When that failed, Islamabad tried to mobilise the refugees themselves, educated in the seminaries and *madrasehs* of the frontier provinces, to seize power in Kabul behind the banner of Taliban. However, Islamabad's hope of being able to control the Taliban came to nothing, for the Taliban regime, having come to power, had no desire the play to Islamabad's tunes. Hence, when Washington launched its War on Terror against the Taliban regime in Kabul, Islamabad was merely abandoning non-performing assets.

The Karzai administration that the US helped put in power in Kabul has not always played this role for Islamabad,[41] which goes quite a long way in explaining why the ISI continues to carry out or support stealth operations in Afghanistan (such as the attack on the Indian Embassy in Kabul). This is largely because given the shambles the Afghan economy has been reduced to, it would be quite a challenge to provide economic opportunities for the people who are now actually inside the country, let alone for refugees returning home. Hence, the Karzai administration, just like the Taliban before it, has been not particularly keen on settling the issue of repatriation in Islamabad's favour right away. This in turn makes Islamabad, and particularly the military establishment, to try manoeuvres beyond their mandate as allies of the USA and NATO in Afghanistan, playing a hand that frequently invites stern criticism from Washington D.C.—such as the alleged support that Pakistan extends to the Haqqani network, and some elements of the Taliban who have no desire to make peace with the Karzai administration.[42]

The ascendancy of the Taliban in Afghanistan backed by Islamabad, the end of the Taliban adventure and then its resurgence-complicated matters inside Pakistan as well. The rise of the Taliban in the late 1990s required not merely the material assistance of the ISI, but also the human support provided by Pakistani militant groups, aiming at the foundation of an Islamic state in Kabul, as a prelude for doing the same in Pakistan. The defeat of Taliban pushed back both these groups back into Pakistan, inviting US military action against the Taliban on Pakistani soil. From the days of Musharraf, the Pakistani government too has come under tremendous pressure from the US to crackdown on these militant Islamist organisations, borne out by the military expeditions in Khyber Pakhtunkhwa and FATA.[43]

Till such time as the Pakistan government and/or the ISI had provided material support or resorted to benign negligence towards these groups, they seldom targeted the Islamabad government. However, once the crackdowns began, the gloves came off—the first evidence of which came in the siege of Lal Masjid in Lahore, in the heart of Punjab. It is largely in this backdrop that forces like Baitullah Mehsud and the Tehrik-e Taliban occurred with the twin agenda of opposition to US presence in Afghanistan and Pakistan, and the foundation of an Islamic order (characterised by a redistributive economic agenda, regulated social order).[44] Such forces gained support among a large array of Islamist forces, demanding immediate withdrawal of the US forces from the region, and strict implementation of the Shari'ah, that is, Nizam-e Mustafa. This new development lies behind the increasing cycle of religious and sectarian violence in urban, and even cosmopolitan, Pakistan.[45]

Islamabad, therefore, needs a regime that is not merely friendly, but also mindful of Pak predicament more than anything else—hence, its determination to maintain some kind of presence in the politics of Afghanistan

Conclusion: Would Pakistan Exit Afghanistan?
The experience of last three decades has clearly shown that the lack of stability in Afghanistan has wider consequences for its neighbours

in West, South, and Central Asia, which explains why Istanbul was chosen as the venue for latest round of deliberations on Afghanistan (2012). For many observers of Afghanistan, the right and proper tone for the talks was set by Turkey's clear and categorical condemnation of the destabilising role ISI plays in Kabul, a charge that Pakistan denies in a very unconvincing manner. A consensus appears to be developing, outside Islamabad as much as in it that Pakistan must exit from Afghanistan and desist from interfering from Afghan domestic politics for the region to stabilise in the medium run.

There can be little disagreement where Pakistan's withdrawal from Afghanistan is concerned; also, it should leave the Afghans to their own devices (perhaps for the first time in its history). However, the more important question is, would it do so? The umbilical cord that ties Pakistan with Afghanistan has become badly entangled, and is very unlikely to be easily severed because the Afghan tragedy of the past three decades has disfigured Pakistan no less than it has Afghanistan.

Islamabad has remained moored in Afghanistan, right from the days of Soviet invasion, through the period of the civil war and then the Taliban. Now that the prospect of US withdrawal from Afghanistan looms large, Islamabad (and particularly the military, and more specifically the ISI) appears to be following a policy of running with the hare and hunting with the hound—cooperating with the US programme for stabilising the Karzai government, and simultaneously opening a back channel with the Taliban.

It is important to stress Islamabad's own requirement for a stable Afghanistan to emerge, for if Afghanistan remains unstable, it might turn out to be merely a matter of time that the Pathans on either side of the Durand line revive the call for an independent Pakhtunistan. Should it emerge, the very existence of Pakistan would be at stake, because given the changing demographic landscape of Pakistan the demand would not affect only Khyber-Pakhtunkhwa region, but also parts of Baluchistan and Punjab on account of the inland migration that has taken place since 1980. Further, such a demand would fuel the increasingly militant secessionism in Baluchistan as well. Thus, it is very unlikely that in the medium term Islamabad would want to settle in favour of any regime that it has no stake in.

The American formulation of the problem as AfPak goes some distance in speaking of not merely combating militancy in the region, but also providing economic assistance to Pakistan alongside the reconstruction of Afghanistan. But as this essay has tried to argue, any international arrangement for the stabilisation of Afghanistan is almost doomed from the very beginning, unless it calibrates the matter of repatriation of Afghan refugees from Pakistan with the reconstruction of Afghanistan. This is not to argue that Islamabad should be given a veto in the process, nor is it to argue that Islamabad's preoccupations should be given priority over those of Kabul. This is merely to make the case that if Islamabad's concerns are not, (and not seen to be) addressed, then Islamabad is very likely to throw a spanner in the wheel, and there would not be much stability in the foreseeable future if that were to happen.

Notes
1. *New York Times*, February 24, 2008.
2. Farhan Bokhari and James Lamont, "Transcript: Interview with Asif Ali Zardari", *the Financial Times*, September 15, 2009. http://www.ft.com/intl/cms/s/0/36a57efa-a205-11de-81a6-00144feabdc0.html#axzz2G1jciZnL (Accessed on December 25, 2012).
3. Speaking at the first Presidential Debate in October 2008, Obama argued that the Afghan situation should not be treated in isolation, because Taliban and al-Qaeda operatives were proven to be hiding in 'safe havens in Pakistan.' "Transcript of the First Presidential Debate", *CNN*, October 14, 2008. http://edition.cnn.com/2008/POLITICS/09/26/debate.mississippi.transcript/ (Accessed on December 25, 2012).
4. "In India, Karzai reaches out to 'brother' Pakistan", *Reuters*, October 05, 2011. http://www.reuters.com/article/2011/10/05/us-afghanistan-india-idUSTRE79417D20111005 (Accessed on December 25, 2012).

5. Thomas Barfield, *Afghanistan: A Cultural and Political History*, (Princeton: Princeton University Press, 2010), p. 154.
6. Daveed Gartenstein-Ross and Tara Vassefi, "The Forgotten History of Afghanistan-Pakistan Relations," Yale *Journal of International Affairs*, March 2012, p. 40.
7. Khurshid Hasan, "Pakistan-Afghanistan Relations," *Asian Survey*, 2(7), 1962, p. 15.
8. Ibid. p. 16.
9. Gartenstein-Ross and Vassefi, op. cit. p. 40.
10. Ibid. p. 42.
11. Technically, Pakistani census does not recognise ethnicity, and identifies only speech groups. Linguistically, Baluchistan has three dominant speech groups, Baluch, Pushtu and Brahui. In the Census, however, Baluch and Brahui are calculated together, producing a figure of 55%, completely effacing the existence of the Brahui speakers who have constituted historically constituted nearly a fifth of the people of the region. For a detailed updated report on the province, see C. Christine Fair, *Baluchistan*, [Report for US House of Representatives, Committee on Foreign Affairs, Oversight and Investigations sub-committee, February 08, 2012]. http://foreignaffairs.house.gov/112/HHRG-112-FA-WState-CFair-20120208.pdf (Accessed on December 25, 2012).
12. Data derived from the Population Association of Pakistan. http://www.pap.org.pk/statistics/population.htm
13. Katherine Adeney, *Federalism and Ethnic Regulation in India and Pakistan*. (new York: Palgrave Macmillan, 2007), p. 149.
14. Ibid. p. 149.
15. Rizwan Hussain, *Pakistan and the Emergence of Islamic Militancy in Afghanistan*, (Hampshire: Ashgate Publishing, 2005), p. 78.
16. Gartenstein-Ross and Vassefi, op. cit. p. 43.
17. Ibid. p. 43.
18. A.Z. Hilali, *US-Pakistan Relationship: Soviet Invasion of Afghanistan*, (Hampshire: Ashgate Publishing, 2005), p. 104.
19. Ian Talbot, *Pakistan: A Modern History*, (New Delhi: Foundation Books, 2005), p. 249.
20. M.G. Weinbaum, "The Politics of Afghan Resettlement and Rehabilitation", *Asian Survey*, 29, no. 3, (March 1989), p. 299.
21. Pervez Iqbal Cheema, "The Afghanistan Crisis and Pakistan's Security Dilemma," *Asian Survey*, 23, no. 3, (March 1983), p. 235.
22. The urban population of Sind climbed from 29.9% to 48.8%; that of Punjab from 17.4% to 13.3%.

23. Mohammad A. Qadeer, *Pakistan: Social and Cultural Transformations in a Muslim Nation*, (London and New York: Routledge, 2006), p. 50.
24. There are also the other routes to 'urbanisation.' Much of the changes in the landscape of Baluchistan region is on account of the massive refugee influx fleeing the Afghan wars in the 1980s, 1990s and after 2002.
25. Qadeer, op. cit. p. 51.
26. Ibid. p. 84.
27. http://www.khyberpakhtunkhwa.gov.pk/aboutus/Area-Population.php [accessed 26th December, 2012.
28. Dr. Habib ur-Rahman, *The Problem of Unemployment in Pakistan: a Case Study of Khyber Pakhtunkhwwah*. http://suit.edu.pk/MGMT/wp-content/uploads/2011/11/The-Problem-of-Unemployment-in-Pakistan-refrsh-upto29-10-11.pdf (Accessed on December 26, 2012).
29. http://balochistan.gov.pk/mics/MICS-4-Web/4-7-Results-NIC-TB-Unemployment-HH%20Asset.pdf
30. http://www.pdma.gov.pk/PaRRSA/documents/PCNA_Report/Chapter3_Strategic_Objective2.pdf
31. Qadeer, op. cit. p. 84.
32. Pakistan today has a gini concentration ratio of over 30.6. The poorest 10% of the people contribute to only 3.9% of the national income, while the richest 10% put in over 26%. https://www.cia.gov/library/publications/the-world-factbook/geos/pk.html
33. http://www.khyberpakhtunkhwa.gov.pk/Departments/PnD/mne/MnE/Download/7.%20PCNA%20Report.pdf
34. Ali Riaz, *Faithful Education: Madrassahs in South Asia*, (New Brunswick, NJ and London: Rutgers University Press, 2008), p. 79.
35. Ibid. p. 92.
36. Of particular significance was Zia's undermining of the judiciary in Pakistan by introducing Shari'ah benches in the four provincial High Courts in 1979, with the power to annul any law found repugnant to Islam, followed by their replacement in 1981 with the appointment of *'ulema* as judges, for the first time in the history of Pakistan. The objective of erecting an Islamic judiciary parallel to the one instituted by the constitution continued in 1984 with the creation of Qazi to courts to operate at the local level. For a reasonably comprehensive treatment of the Islamisation programme under Zia, see Talbot, op. cit. pp. 270-83.
37. Riaz, op. cit. p 113-14.
38. Talbot, op.cit. p. 340.
39. Riaz, op. cit. p. 94.
40. Ibid. p. 95.

41. See for instance, Tahir Khan, "Afghanistan rejects repatriation deadline extension," *The Tribune*, December 22, 2012. http://tribune.com.pk/story/482695/afghanistan-rejects-repatriation-deadline-extension/ (Accessed on December 26, 2012).
42. See for instance, Philip J Quinlan, Pakistan: A Conflicted Ally in the Fight against Terrorism, *Global Security Studies*, Winter 2012, vol. 3, no. 1. http://globalsecuritystudies.com/Quinlan%20Pakistan%20Final.pdf (Accessed on December 26, 2012).
43. Musharraf himself spoke of the infamous threat made by US deputy secretary of state, Richard Armitage, that USA would "bomb Pakistan back to the stone age" if it did not reorient Pakistani foreign policy away from the Taliban. See, Pervez Musharraf, *In the Line of Fire: A Memoir*, (New York: Free Press, 2006), p. 201; cited in Gartenstein-Ross and Vassefi, op. cit. p. 44.
44. Syed Farooq Hasnat, "Pakistan's Strategic Interests: Afghanistan and the Fluctuating US Strategy," *Journal of International Affairs*, Fall/Winter 2009, vol. 63, no. 1, p. 148.
45. For a good account of this phenomenon, see Riaz, op. cit. pp. 108-115.

4. Dragon Splashing the Muddy Water: China in South Asian Region

Binoda kumar Mishra

The former US president Bill Clinton once termed South Asia as the most dangerous place on earth. He referred to the existence of nuclear weapons in the region under the possession of two feuding countries such as India and Pakistan and the prospect of them being used. Thankfully, Clinton's apprehension has not come anywhere closer in reality. But naïve would it be to say that South Asia is not the most dangerous place on the earth; dangerous not so much due to the existence of nuclear weapons but due to the existence of non-state actors posing threat to state-system in a part of the region— Afghanistan-Pakistan (AfPak). Afghanistan, a largely forgotten nation after the Soviet withdrawal from that country, started bearing the fruits of the mindless balancing acts of the superpowers. Forces created by the United States with the help of Pakistani authorities and Chinese weapons to fight the Soviets in Afghanistan emerged with their own identity as dangerous forces to reckon with. The fullest expression of that danger was realised only when the most powerful state was spectacularly attacked inside its own territory. World attention turned towards Afghanistan making it the theatre of war on terror. Pakistan, the part sinner in the past in creating this danger, was forced to cooperate with the US led war on terror with the threat of obliteration if it refused compliance. Until around 2006, the problem was seen as a problem limited to Afghanistan and needed to be tackled in that State with the help of Pakistan. Soon it was realised that the foci of terror in Afghanistan is as much in Pakistan as it is in Afghanistan. The theatre expanded to be called as AfPak theatre. The NATO led International Security Assistance Force is engaged in a bitter battle causing collateral casualties to the civilians through ground operations in Afghanistan and through drone attacks in the Federally Administered Tribal Areas of Pakistan. Though there has been a declaration by the US to withdraw its and NATO troops by the end of 2014, the ground reality is yet to come anywhere close to conducive for such withdrawal.

Conjectures are rife as to what would happen in the post-2014 scenario. These conjectures are not limited to the possible internal scenario in Afghanistan but also regarding the future role of major powers involved and likely to be involved in the region or have a stake in the region. China is one such power having both the ability and reasons to be involved in the region. In terms of ability, it has both the economic and military ability to take over the role now being played by the US in the region and in terms of reason, it has plenty of strategic considerations that demand close Chinese involvement. However, China does not fit into any conventional description of sovereign State and its foreign policy. It has the reputation of planning for long and the dubious reputation of unilaterally pursuing her goals in defiance of international norms and concerns and her role in the region, till date, is a classic case of the latter approach.

As mentioned above the cheaper Chinese weapons were used to arm the religiously motivated Talibs easily to launch a jihad against the Soviets. This was a token contribution of China to this region during the past superpower rivalry. Apart from that, China herself, in her considered national interest invested a bit in the region. The investment was in the form of preparing a State strong enough to stand up to the might of India which it considers as its 'long-term potential adversary'.[1] It all began after the Sino-Indian war of 1962. One can see China devising a long-term strategy to extend her influence in

South Asia unmindful of the consequences for the region and for the international community as a whole. China's involvement in South Asia began as an invitation from Pakistan that emerged out of India and was always in crisis of identity. From then till date, China plays her strategies mindlessly with the intent of benefitting from this region. With inherent interstate problems, the already muddy region had the effect of being further muddied, as Chinese actions have only aggravated the problem with dire consequences to the region and outside world. The Chinese role and its effects have two direct results, viz. making the region most dangerous in terms of interstate relationships, and strengthening non-state actors posing a threat to the state system in the region.

China Factor in South Asian Inter-state Relations
In the Indo-centric region of South Asia, India by virtue of her size, scale of economy, democratic traditions, and moderate economic prowess is imagined as the natural leader of the region. However, the historic partition of the sub-continent on religious lines that created India and Pakistan, generated in the latter the anxiety of being swallowed by mighty India. Thus, emerging as strong as India became a national pursuit for the Pakistani leadership. India on the other hand was choosing a path that would take India to her deserving position of a benevolent world leader. Nevertheless, the realities of prevailing international circumstances forced India to embrace power in its ultimate form. A nation that came into being on the plank of non-violence and preached non-alignment had to pursue power in all its forms including the nuclear weapons. It can be argued that in the sharply divided Cold War international order, Non-Aligned India had no such pressing compulsions of pursuing nuclear weapons. However, a brief discussion on India's road to nuclear weapons would make it clear that it was not so much the compulsions of Cold War as much as China that was responsible

for India to adopt the nuclear path at very early stages of her independent existence. Though it was Nehru's personal preference that India should possess nuclear weapons capability, he did not clearly articulate under what circumstances should India go nuclear. He initiated a massive scientific research that can be directed towards weaponisation. Despite having all the preparedness for going overtly nuclear by the year 1966, India chose not to cross the threshold till 1998. The decision to go the weapons way can only be explained by Chinese approach towards the region.

China played her role during this period through helping Pakistan that was desperate to procure nuclear weapons. Any nationalistic Indian would call Pakistan's nuclear programme as an aggressive posture vis-a-vis India but an objective analysis of Pakistani nuclear project would certainly conclude that Pakistan was well within its right to pursue a nuclear programme in reference to Indian nuclear programme. The logic for Pakistan was simple and remains so. Given the history of war and constant conflict with India, Pakistan needed an insurance against Indian nuclear weapons. In the words of a Pakistani General, "[s]ome safety against extinction is the inalienable right of an individual or a nation. Oxygen is basic to life, and one does not debate its desirability ... nuclear deterrence has assumed that life-saving property for Pakistan."[2] This is what Herbert Butterfield calls security dilemma as Hobbesian fear. Despite the fact, as it has been seen, that India never intended to do Pakistan any harm unless provoked, Pakistan was justified in suffering from the sensation of nakedness vis-à-vis Indian conventional and nuclear capability. This situation is a typical security dilemma as Butterfield informs us. Butterfield writes:

> "It is this peculiar characteristic of the situation that I am describing ... that you yourself may vividly feel the terrible fear that you have of the other party, but you cannot enter into the other man's counter-fear, or

even understand why he should be particularly nervous. For you know that you yourself mean no harm, and that you want nothing from him save guarantees for your own safety; and it is never possible for you to realise or remember properly that since he cannot see the inside of your mind, he can never have the same assurance of your intensions that you have."[3]

In a timeline, one can see the evolution of Pakistan's nuclear programme. Pakistan embarked on her nuclear programme in 1951 for peaceful purposes. The programme showed interest in nuclear weapons only as a reaction to India's nuclear weapons programme. The relation is evident from the fact that Pakistan expressed her interest to sign the Nuclear Non-Proliferation Treaty (NPT) but with the condition that India does so. In the 16th annual session of the United Nations Atomic Energy Conference held in Mexico in September 1972, Pakistan put forward the proposal to denuclearise South Asia.[4] Again, Pakistan repeated the proposal in 1974 but India did not respond.[5] There are scholars who argue that Pakistan's pledge to denuclearise South Asia was a camouflage for her weapons programme. Such an interpretation is more a matter of conjecture than analysis. A better interpretation of Pakistani nuclear abolition proposal is that Pakistan knew fully well that she was in a position of weakness in relation to India, and thus wanted to prevent India from possessing nuclear weapons. Had India accepted the Pakistani proposals, the latter would not have pursued the costly nuclear weapons programme. Secondly, India's nuclear programme created a nuclear circle around herself. India's refusal to sign the NPT and subsequent conduct of the PNE made Pakistan desperate. From a position of nuclear abolition, Pakistan started pursuing an aggressive nuclear programme only to counter the Indian nuclear and conventional threat. If India was justified in pursuing a nuclear weapons programme against uncertain Chinese nuclear and conventional posture, then Pakistan was equally justified in pursuing a protective nuclear cover for herself. In its endeavour to obtain the nuclear capability Pakistan looked at the enemy of its enemy, that is, China.

In an attempt to develop deterrent nuclear capability, Pakistan walked into the strategic sphere of China. From 1965 till 1976 Pakistan kept pleading for Chinese help. Zulfikar Ali Bhutto travelled three times to China between 1971 and 1976 only to obtain Chinese assistance for nuclear weapons technology.[6] China took some time to assess the prospects and consequences of supporting Pakistan. Finally, once it was convinced about Pakistan's loyalties, China agreed to help Pakistan in developing the nuclear programme. The Sino-Pakistan collaboration began from 1976 indicating that such partnership was a reaction to India's 1974 PNE. This provided China with a great opportunity to encircle India with nuclear weapons. China, though a party to NPT chose to violate its provisions in full knowledge of the US and the international community and assisted Pakistan.[7] The Chinese help in terms of technology was not going to be sufficient for developing the weapons. It needed huge money that Pakistan was in no position to afford. It was at this point, Pakistan developed the civilisational logic to mobilise fund. The term 'Islamic bomb' appealed to the Arab world that poured money, which went into the Pakistani nuclear programme. China found this to be an easy way to increase her sphere of influence in the whole of Asia. Through the support to Pakistan nuclear programme China intended to befriend the entire Islamic world that would remain indebted to China. Indeed, it is not clear how much obligation does China actually command from the Islamic world on this account, but it is her help to the 'Islamic bomb' project that has added a non-state dimension to the South Asian nuclear complex.

The second nuclear phase that led to nuclearisation of both India and Pakistan in 1998 was also related to the Chinese actions. I have argued in details elsewhere that India's May 1998 test was in response to concrete Chinese actions during 1993 to 1995.[8] In a series of activities, China violated international non-proliferation norms and supported Pakistan's nuclear weapons programme along with stationing nuclear missiles in the caves of Tibet that can arguably have no target other than India.[9] This nuclear aggression compelled India to cross the nuclear threshold and bury the age-old ambiguity on nuclear weapons. This of course led to tests by Pakistan that was ready with Chinese-aided device. Thus, South Asia emerged as the newest nuclear flashpoint with bitter rivals possessing nuclear weapons. Pakistan's possession of nuclear weapons may be looked as the right of any sovereign nation to possess them in accordance with their threat perception, but the trouble is that one cannot be sure of Pakistan remaining under rational control. Moreover, the more vulnerable the Pakistani state becomes to non-state actors, greater the dangers of these nuclear weapons reaching the non-state actors that have been empowered by the US money, Pakistan's logistics, and Chinese weapons. These radical forces created during the height of Cold War to be used as pawns against the former Soviet Union became independent as soon as the US turned its face from Afghanistan post the Soviet withdrawal. The Islamic identity that was used to motivate the refugees from Afghanistan in Pakistan now became the basis for global jihad against the free world. Fatal combination of State and non-State actors emerged in Afghanistan that challenged concepts of democracy and human rights not only Afghanistan but also in the neighbouring areas and expressed the intention of challenging the free world all over the globe.

Immediate important neighbours such as India, China, and Pakistan had different interests in the region and different compulsions/strategies in dealing with Afghanistan. India being opposed to the forces capturing power in Afghanistan chose to sever all ties with Afghanistan; Pakistan on the other hand looked at the situation as a strategic opportunity to extend her influence over the radically charged Islamist forces and to use Afghanistan to increase its strategic depth. China on her own, though was apprehensive of the fallout of encouraging the radical forces in Afghanistan, and was in no position to differentiate her interests from the interests of her *all weather* friend, Pakistan. China saw the interests of Pakistan somehow converging with at least one of her interests, that is, bullying India either through the Pakistan State or through non-state forces created by Pakistan in Pakistan and Afghanistan. This convergence of interests made China clandestinely support Pakistan's strategic cosiness with radical forces of Afghanistan and parts of Pakistan. China earnestly hoped that Pakistan would and more importantly would be able to protect Chinese interests in the region.

As it developed, the non-state actors charged with radical Islamist ideology and equipped with Chinese weapons and Pakistani military training had developed their own minds and had started calculating their own interests (global jihad) above all others. In the post-9/11 scenario, when Pakistan was arm twisted by the US to join the war on terror launched by the US, China certainly sided with the US in convincing Pakistan to come over to the side of war on terror. This changed the strategic scenario in the region. Pakistan joining the US in the war on terror brought reprisal from the radical forces onto Pakistan itself. Discussing the Chinese situation Andrew Small writes, "That protected status of Chinese interests in Pakistan has gone. As Pakistan's government has become a target, so has China. Chinese workers have been variously kidnapped and executed in Dir, Peshawar, and Islamabad as jihadi groups seek to weaken the central state and the bases of its external support."[10] China now has to recast her strategies and policies to protect a host of her interests; Michael D. Swaine identifies them, "(a) its intimate and long-standing ties to (and potential influence upon) Pakistan, (b) its ongoing geostrategic interests vis-à-vis the two most important local powers active in Central and South Asia (Russia and especially India), (c) its deepening political and economic involvement in Central Asia,

(d) its growing concern over the link between Central and South Asian terrorism and Muslim insurgents and terrorists in Xinjiang and elsewhere within China, (e) its bilateral relationship with the US, and (f) its energy and mineral interests in Afghanistan."[11]

Of the six important Chinese motivations, Swaine identifies a friendly relationship or influence over Pakistan is primary among Chinese interests.[12] It is a fact that Chinese strategy towards South Asia aims at best to establish Chinese hegemony over the region or at the least to contain the rise of India. Pakistan, thus, fits to the Chinese scheme of things. Pakistan has enjoyed Chinese support all through her independent existence to act as a proxy to China in attempting to deter India's growing influence in the region. When it comes to the contemporary situation in the AfPak region, China, like Pakistan, grows anxious over India's increasing importance in Afghanistan. India, like China, has not committed active troops in Afghanistan but has been involved in a big way in reconstructing Afghanistan. India is among the largest civilian donors into Afghanistan. It is the sixth largest bilateral donor. All of India's involvement is directed towards capacity building of the Afghan people that can have long-term impact on Afghanistan-India relationship. This increasing profile of India in Afghanistan is a cause of concern primarily for Pakistan and by extension and directly for China. It is noteworthy that China is only the second non-western country to sign a strategic partnership with Afghanistan following India's strategic partnership agreement with Afghanistan.[13]

Realising Pakistan's increasing inability in protecting China's interested in Pakistan and in Afghanistan, China has embarked upon a dual strategy to protect her own interests in the region. It does support Pakistan and Pakistan's agenda insofar as it is directed against India. One may recall that after the attack in Mumbai, when India produced dossier of evidence against specific persons and organisations operating from within Pakistan, to be behind the attack and cornering Pakistan to act against such people and organisations, only China that went to protect Pakistan in the UN, and other international bodies. As Ayesha Siddiqua notes, "Beijing has also engaged in direct negotiations and deals with right-wing religious parties and groups like the Pakistan-based Jamaat-e-Islami and Jamaat-ud-Dawwa. In case of the latter, China, on the behest of Pakistan, blocked any adverse move in the UN Security Council against the JuD."[14]

Secondly, China does not hesitate to continue supporting Pakistani dual faced nuclear programme despite clear vulnerabilities of her nuclear establishments to the attacks of rogue non-state actors. It has been reported by many independent sources that there have been near successful attacks on Pakistani nuclear establishments.[15] It goes on to show China's Pakistan-first approach towards South Asia. From the Indian standpoint, one certainly fails to see reason in such Chinese approach towards Pakistan. Equipping a vulnerable country with dangerous equipments that can reach the hands of the deadliest non-state actors who hardly distinguish among their targets is certainly an inexplicable act about which China has failed to convince the international community. The intriguing fact is that China does this knowing fully well the prospects of these weapons getting into the hands of the Islamist nexus that have started operating in China's Xinjiang province.

China Wins, No Matter Who Loses?
China now chooses to deal directly with Afghanistan to protect her material interests in that country which includes rich resources. China is walking a tight rope of dual interests, viz. to keep Pakistan under its influence and at the same time effectively protect her own interests in Afghanistan. These two objectives may seem contradictory, as the Afghan authorities are increasingly growing suspicious of the Pakistani authorities, particularly the military. Therefore, keeping

Pakistan happy and pursuing China's interests in Afghanistan may sound a parallel track approach with no converging point but China finds a converging point. China very well understands that her interests in the whole of Afghanistan cannot be protected only through the established government in Kabul as the latter's writ is very limited in the country. Large part of Afghanistan is under *de facto* control of various insurgent and local militia groups. Thus, there exists a convergence between two of China's objectives. Known for its little respect to international norms and concerns, China unhesitatingly cultivates the militias whenever it is required to carry out Chinese projects in Afghanistan.

Siddiqua further notes:

> "Sources also point fingers towards the fact that the Taliban present in Nooristan (Pakistan) have not tried to obstruct the Chinese presence in nearby Gilgit-Baltistan. This, they believe, indicates some form of tacit understanding between the two sets of actors. In this regard, this approach may have long term implications, as these partners could work as a buffer in the AfPak region between China and its competitors like India."[16]

By cultivating the local militias and the insurgents, China indirectly supports Pakistan's cause in Afghanistan. At the same time, through engagement with the Afghan government, China wins large projects of resource extraction. Most visible are the Aynak Copper mine and its associated transport and electricity-generating facility in the Logar province making it the largest foreign direct investment in Afghanistan.[17]

During the recent visit of Zhou Yongkang, a member of the CCP's politburo standing committee in September 2012, China pledged, among other things, to train, fund and equip Afghan security forces. This gesture of the Chinese has gone down well with the Afghan government as well as the US. China, which did not commit any troops to fighting the insurgents in Afghanistan despite having the capacity to do so, is now more than eager to train, equip and fund the security forces in line with India's engagement. This clearly shows China's intent to replace India as the dominant contributor to Afghanistan in security matters. The Chinese motive can be analysed in both simple and a complex manner. In simple terms, it is just an attempt to prevent India from growing her influence over Afghanistan particularly in the post-US withdrawal phase, and to strengthen a case for early exit of the US. However, it is well known that the volatility of the Afghan situation is far from over and in case the US actually withdraws in 2014, there is a strong chance of the radical forces capturing power in Afghanistan. This future prognosis is something that both the US and the Chinese are dreading. Apart from the obvious US concerns, China has every reason to fear for an Islamist alliance working against China inside China in its Xinjiang province. So the other way of looking at China extending its help to train, fund and equip the Afghan security forces while cultivating the insurgents is as an attempt to prepare for any direction Afghanistan takes in the post withdrawal phase. If it emerges as a stable country with a strong central rule, China will have substantial influence on the government and its military. Moreover, if it lapses into chaos with all the insurgent groups and the local militias fighting for power, China still protects her interests by dint of having maintained a good relationship with them.

Does it mean that China completely dropped Pakistan from its priorities? Certainly not as Pakistan is and will remain important to China's domestic security and regional strategic calculations. First, in line of China's emerging profile as a big power, China requires huge resources to for her domestic civilian and military requirements. Both Afghanistan and Pakistan are crucial to China in this respect. According to various sources, Pakistan has impressive natural resources including copper (around 200 billion tons), zinc, and aluminium and lead that China eyes to tap. Beijing has bagged important mining contracts in Saidek of Baluchistan and is all set to win another mining contract, allegedly unscrupulously, the Riko Dik mining project. Apart from these, Chinese interest in ensuring secured energy route through Gwadar port and various mining and construction activity in Gilgit-Baltistan area. Thus, Pakistan remains crucial for Chinese interests, both economic and strategic.

Similarly, as indicated earlier, China also has serious economic interests in Afghanistan as well. 'Both Afghanistan and Pakistan fall in the belt of the 'Tethyan Magmatic Arc', which extends from Mongolia to Pakistan to Turkey and carries minerals like copper, gold, zinc, lead, iron ore, aluminium, etc'.[18] China, mindful of her domestic resource requirement, has gone ahead in engaging the Afghan government independent of Pakistan indicating China's crave for resources and the means China can adopt to rationalise resource security for itself. However, China is not unaware of the negative ramifications of an Afghanistan ruled by radical forces. It certainly fears the radical Islamist forces joining hands in escalating violence in Muslim dominated provinces such as Xinjiang.

To prevent the movements such as that of the Uyghurs from being connected with the global jihadi network China needs the help of Pakistan at one level and the US at another. Thus, there also exist a convergence of interests between the US and China in the region as neither of the two wish to see the region lapse into the lawless rule of the radical forces. However, the question is, what happens if it does lapse as is being feared to be the most likely scenario post-ISAF withdrawal? Knowing Pakistani establishment's patronage towards the militants operating from the AfPak region, China sees Pakistan as the key to prevent these militants from helping the Uyghur movement in Xinjiang province and elsewhere in China. Nevertheless, the recent developments inside Pakistan indicate that Pakistan may be losing the influence it had over the militant forces it created and extends patronage. The situation seems to have been reversed where the militants are seeming to exert influence over Pakistan polity either though ideology or through interest convergence against India or though violent means of attacking Pakistan civilian leadership and general citizens. China realises the futility of depending too much on Pakistan to ensure immunity from Islamist intervention inside China. Thus, the US in its present role is a plausible alternative for China. What China wishes the US to do is not remain in the region for too long but leave crippling the militant forces' ability to an extent that they never emerge a dictating force in the region and do not capture power in Afghanistan or in Pakistan. The near sure withdrawal of the US by 2014 increases Chinese anxieties regarding the ability of the Afghan forces to deter the militants that are not decimated. Therefore, we see China committing to intervene in Afghanistan by means of training and equipping the Afghan security forces without committing troops to combat the militants. The logic is one of free riding. The US and other NATO forces, China expects, to disarm the militants substantially so that they are unable to come to the centre stage.

China on the other hand does not wish to antagonise Pakistan and thus would have to allow Pakistan pursing her strategic interests in Afghanistan though keeping alive the strategically useful militant force. China hopes her cultivation of the militants in the periphery, as part of her practical economic engagement, would be sufficient to control these forces and prevent them from joining the Uyghur movement in China direct their activities towards India, the common strategic adversary of China and Pakistan in the region and beyond. It thus can be concluded that China has adopted a strategy that practically ensures Chinese interests in the region in whatever scenario that emerges post

2014. However, one cannot be sure if the region will experience peace and stability and if the practical approach of the Chinese yield the desired results for the region and for China itself. If history of the region is anything to go by it is evident that the non-state actors mobilised as a force have bitten the hand that fed them. The US-Pakistan created Taliban is now the deadliest enemy of the US and the limited secular, democratic fabric of Pakistan. Thus one can only conclude that Chinese double game of siding with the US and engaging the Afghan central government while cultivating, along with Pakistan, the radically charged militant forces is a dangerous game of splashing mud, and thinking it would not soil her clothes.

Notes

1. *Can the Chinese Army Win the Next War?* (Beijing: Central Military Commission, 1993), Cited in Ashok Kapur, "China and the Proliferation: Implications for India," *China Report*, vol.34, nos.3-4, December 1998, pp. 403-04.
2. Gen Mirza Aslam Beg, "Pakistan's Nuclear Imperatives," *National Development and Security*, vol. 3, no. 10, November 1994, pp. 29-41. Quoted in Manpreet Sethi, *Nuclear Strategy: India's March towards Credible Deterrence*, (New Delhi: KW Publishers and CAPS, 2009), p. 45.
3. Herbert Butterfield, *History of Human Relations*, (London: Collins, 1951), p. 21.
4. *Dawn*, October 04, 1972, cited by Savita Pande, "Nuclear Weapon-Free Zone in South Asia", *Strategic Analysis*, vol. 22, no. 11, February 1999, p. 1681.
5. General Assembly draft resolution, a/C.1/L.682.
6. Zulfikar Ali Bhutto terms the China-Pakistan bilateral nuclear agreement as historic and his greatest achievement and contribution to the survival of Pakistani people and Pakistan nation. Zulfikar Ali Bhutto, *If I am Assassinated*, (New Delhi: Vikas, 1979), p. 138.
7. Ashok Kapur, *Pokhran and Beyond: India's Nuclear Behaviour*, (New Delhi: Oxford University Press, 2001), p. 194.
8. Binoda Kumar Mishra, "China Factor in South Asia's Nuclear Politics," in Bhumitra Chakma (ed.), *Politics of Nuclear Weapons in South Asia*, (Surrey: Ashgate Publishing Ltd., 2011).
9. Ibid

10. Andrew Small, "China's AfPak Moment". http://www.gmfus.org/galleries/ct_publication_attachments/Small_AfPak_Brief_0509_final.pdf
11. Michael D. Swaine, "China and the "AfPak" Issue," *China Leadership Monitor*, no. 31, February 15, 2010, p. 2.
12. Ibid.
13. C Raja Mohan, "Approaching Kabul," *The Indian Express*, September 25, 2012. http://www.indianexpress.com/news/approaching-kabul/1007272/0
14. Ayesha Siddiqua, "Expansion by Stealth: China's Interests, Infrastructure & Investments in Pakistan & Afghanistan," *CIDOB Policy Research Project*, p. 6. http://www.cidob.org/en/temas_regiones/asia/sources_of_tension_in_afghanistan_pakistan_regional_perspectives. Also see, http://www.indianexpress.com/news/wikileaks-china-thwarted-action-against-antiindia-terrorists/721031/0; and http://pakteahouse.net/2009/07/15/jamaat-e-islami-and-the-chinese-communist-party/
15. For an account of these attacks see, Binoda Kumar Mishra, Op. Cit.
16. Ayesha Siddiqua, Op. Cit.
17. Michael D. Swaine, Op. Cit., p. 6.
18. Ayesha Siddiqua, Op. Cit., p. 7.

5. India's Afghan Policy: America's Victory to Pakistan's Quagmire

Pramit Palchaudhuri

Over the past 15 years, few countries have seen a manifold increase in Indian interest in its national security and political future than Afghanistan. While it does not share a functional border with India, Afghanistan has come to be seen as an integral part of India's broader neighbourhood policy. It has also come to be an essential subset of New Delhi's policy towards its most difficult foreign policy challenge: its relationship with Pakistan.

However, though Afghanistan's strategic profile has grown immensely in India, New Delhi has found its ability to influence matters in that country to be limited. This is a consequence of a combination of three factors. One is the lack of a physical link between India and Afghanistan, whether by sea or land, or even a direct air passage over strategically neutral territory. The other is a mix of India's limited economic resources and diplomatic capacity. The last is a strong policy inhibition in New Delhi against overseas military involvement by its armed forces, something that considerably constrained its influence in a country at war.

Since 2002, India has pursued its largest overseas assistance and aid programme in Afghanistan, a programme that has become a blueprint for Indian aid activity in other parts of the world. It has also invested more time and effort in reaching out to various sections of Afghan society and its leadership than it has almost any other country.

But the inhibitions and capacity restraints mentioned above have meant that the core of India's pursuit of its Afghan interests has been through the leverage of relations with third countries—most notably riding on the coattails of the US—or the use of Afghanistan to further interests with other countries—most strikingly using the Afghan situation to accelerate the peace process with Pakistan.

There are three distinct phases to India's policy to Afghanistan following the fall of the Taliban regime in 2002:

- The first was defined by what was an effective military partnership with the US designed to overthrow the Taliban regime, reduce Pakistani influence in Afghanistan and undermine the use of Afghanistan as a base for terrorist activity against India.
- The second phase ran between 2008 and 2010. Its leitmotif were Indian fears of a US military withdrawal from Afghanistan and the degree it would undo the security gains that New Delhi had accrued with the fall of the Taliban regime. New Delhi went as far as to conclude a US withdrawal could strategically be to its benefit. The logic—Washington was becoming increasingly absorbed about winning over the Pakistan military through money and weapons to support a post-withdrawal Afghan regime. The fallout was a paralysed Pakistani democratic polity, increased terrorist activity in the 'AfPak' region and a stalled Indo-Pakistan peace process.
- The last phase resulted from the collapse of US-Pakistani strategic ties following the assassination of Al Qaeda leader and terrorist, Osama bin Laden, inside Pakistan. India came to accept that a US withdrawal would not be as sweeping as originally thought, that a Taliban takeover of Kabul was not imminent and the costs this would impose on Pakistan could be useful to India's own policies regarding Pakistan.

The Partnership: 2001-08

India had been among the governments most hostile to the Taliban regime that took over Afghanistan after the mujahedin civil war that followed the end of Soviet military occupation.

In particular, New Delhi was concerned that Afghanistan, a traditionally friendly country to India, had become a strategic colony of the Pakistani military.[1]

More tangibly, New Delhi believed the Taliban regime provided training bases and revenue through heroin smuggling for terrorist groups like the Lashkar e Toiba and the Jaish e Mohammed that Islamabad directed against India, primarily to further Pakistan's territorial claim on Kashmir. This was privately described by the then Indian foreign minister, Jaswant Singh, as 'the jihad machine'.[2] This allowed Pakistan to sustain terrorist action against India at virtually no financial cost to itself. The use of Afghan territory for much of the infrastructure that supported the Indian Kashmir insurgency also gave Islamabad plausible deniability in response to New Delhi's accusations of "state-sponsored" terrorism.[3]

India had joined Iran and Russia in supporting the Northern Alliance, a motley collection of Afghan mujahedin groups who opposed the Taliban regime. But they posed no serious threat to the Taliban regime and retained control of only a small portion of north-eastern Afghanistan. India otherwise had no instruments to affect the Taliban regime in anyway and the international community, including the US, tended to treat the Kashmir insurgency as a local problem which India should try to solve on its own.

Al Qaeda's attack on the US on September 11, 2001, dramatically changed this state of affairs. As Al Qaeda's leadership, including its head Osama Bin Laden, were based in Afghanistan as guests of the Taliban regime, the US moved to turn its enormous military might against the Islamicist Kabul regime.

India was a strong supporter of US operations against the

Taliban. It fully backed the US's decision to tie-up with the Northern Alliance to spearhead the military operations against the Taliban regime. The then Indian Prime Minister, Atal Bihari Vajpayee, even offered the US the right to use Indian military bases in its fight.

While India's offer was never taken up by the US, New Delhi's overtures did help in persuading Pakistan, otherwise reluctant to provide the US assistance in the overthrow of a regime that was effectively its own protégé, to throw its weight behind the US action.[4]

New Delhi also pushed hard for the administration of President George W. Bush to accept that the 'war on terrorism' would encompass all terrorist groups, not only Al Qaeda and the Taliban but also groups like the Lashkar e Toiba and Jaish e Mohammed. It was an argument that was accepted in principle by Washington in the immediate aftermath of 9/11.

After the fall of the Taliban regime and the establishment of the Hamid Karzai government in Kabul, India launched an Afghanistan aid programme in 2002. India also quietly sounded out the US on the idea of sending Indian troops as part of the international military forces that were being sent to back the Karzai government and keep the Taliban at bay. The Bush administration eventually refused, largely because of strong warnings from Pakistan that if Indian troops became part of the US war effort then Washington would not be able to count on any assistance from Pakistan.[5] Even by then it was clear that the overland supply routes from Pakistan into Afghanistan were essential to sustaining any large US military operations in the latter country.

India's Afghanistan policy was to be a quiet, backbench supporter of the US political and military effort to rebuild Afghanistan and create a stable non-Taliban regime. However, India's efforts were limited in large part anyway because of Pakistan's severe allergy to any action by New Delhi in Afghanistan. India, therefore, concentrated on its aid programme which, over the years, was to expand into the largest foreign assistance commitment in its history. Over the next 10 years, India pledged over US$ 2 billion in assistance to Afghanistan, making it the fifth largest aid donor of the Kabul regime.[6]

India's steadfast support for the US presence was unmoved by the Bush administration's invasion of Iraq, a war that led to more and more US financial and military resources being shifted away from the Afghan front. In 2003, the Pakistani military's Inter-Services Intelligence 'helped the Taliban restart their insurgency in Afghanistan and provided them with the supplies, training camps and infrastructure'.[7] In a few years, a shattered Taliban had begun to regroup and had become a potent threat to the Karzai regime.

New Delhi, nonetheless, continued to feel the US was its only real option in Afghanistan in keeping the Taliban out of power. In 2007, say Indian diplomats, New Delhi turned down an overture from Iran to being cooperating on resurrecting the original Northern Alliance and developing an anti-Taliban force that did not depend on Washington. India's decision was partly driven by its own assessment that the Northern Alliance, shorn of many of its original leaders, was no longer a viable political or military force in Afghanistan. Additionally, New Delhi was pleased at the success of back channel diplomatic negotiations with the then Pakistani leader, General Pervez Musharraf. Part of the success of the talks was assigned to Musharraf's assessment of the state of affairs in Afghanistan.[8]

The Retreat: 2009-10
The double cost of waging war in Iraq and Afghanistan began to weigh on a US that, by 2009, was also struggling with the aftermath of the subprime financial crisis. The Taliban continued to gain strength on the ground in Afghanistan. There was also a growing rift between Karzai and the US, with the former increasingly worried at whether

Washington had the wherewithal to back him in the long run and the US becoming skeptical of Karzai's ability to ever stitch together a stable Afghan coalition.

The Taliban's return was also a sign that Pakistan was beginning to smell the possibility of a return of its own influence in Afghanistan. The Pakistani military increased its support for the Taliban with the goal of forcing the US and Karzai to accept a Kabul government in which the Taliban played a major role. An additional goal was to force a US military withdrawal from Afghanistan, the calculation being that the resulting vacuum would result in a Taliban victory and a return of Pakistani influence in Afghanistan.

One of the clearest signs of this renewed Pakistani confidence was a suicide bomb attack by a Taliban-related militant group, the Haqqani Network, on the Indian embassy in Kabul in 2008. The US intelligence was able to connect the attack directly to instructions relayed by the Pakistani military's Inter-Services Intelligence. What was striking, however, was the inability of Washington to take any action against Islamabad over the attack. This reflected the US's dependence on Pakistan for the supply routes that sustained the war effort in Afghanistan and, most importantly, a weakening US resolve to continue the war in the country.[9]

The new administration of President Barack Obama had campaigned on the need for a US withdrawal from the Iraq war but had argued that Afghanistan was the 'necessary war'.

Initially, Obama pushed for maintaining the US war effort in Afghanistan but quietly indicated that he wasn't interested in building a 'Jeffersonian democracy' in that country.[10] He appointed one of his foreign policy campaign advisors, Bruce Riedel, to author an Afghanistan policy review. The review supported an increase in the number of US troops fighting in Afghanistan but stressed that Afghanistan-Pakistan were two sides of the same problem— 'AfPak' as it came to be dubbed.

Flowing from this combination of the two countries, Riedel also supported increased US military assistance to Pakistan in an attempt to win some points with Islamabad.[11]

India welcomed the review, which it saw as evidence of consistency in the US Afghan policy. The Indian Ministry of External Affairs said on March 30, 2009, that New Delhi welcomed 'the very clear expression of will to carry through the struggle against extremism in Afghanistan and its roots in Pakistan contained in the new comprehensive US strategy for Afghanistan and Pakistan'. It emphasised that 'India has a direct interest in the success of this international effort'.

However, Obama's support for the troops surge in Afghanistan was really about the president's desire to show domestically that he was prepared to make a last effort at trying to defeat the Taliban. Obama privately would say that he could count on public support for the war for only two years.[12] His underlying view, however, was that the US had to untangle itself from the war and that the heart of the terror problem was really Pakistan. It was a sense that was only strengthened by the US' growing economic problems and declining American public support for the war.

Obama was more transactional about the long-term strategic relationship with India than his predecessor, George W. Bush. During his campaign, the president-to-be had talked of seeking a Kashmir solution—the underlying reason being his aides belief that a Kashmir settlement would make Pakistan more amenable to an Afghan political solution that would allow a US withdrawal. In power, he argued the US had to 'move aggressively on India-Pakistan issues'.[13] India, however, reacted strongly to what is seen as a return to Cold War concepts of South Asian hyphenation. The then Indian National Security Advisor M. K. Narayanan warned that Obama 'was barking up the wrong tree' and New Delhi signalling that it would not accept Kashmir as part of the brief of Obama's Special Envoy for Afghanistan-Pakistan, Richard Holbrooke.[14]

The Indian sense, that the Obama administration was determined to withdraw, and seemed prepared to do so in a manner that would benefit the Taliban and Pakistan, deepened through 2009.

Particular scorn was expressed by Indian officials for Great Britain. After the US, London was the largest provider of foreign troops to the International Security Assistance Force in Afghanistan. But London was desperate to pull its troops out. The term 'British school' became North Block's shorthand for those in the West who wanted a quick and complete military withdrawal from Afghanistan.

The ebb tide for its Afghan policy as far as New Delhi was concerned was the January 2010 London conference where the British government manoeuvred to get the US to commit to a withdrawal. Indian fears were not realized largely thanks to the surprise intervention of the US Secretary of State Hillary Clinton who made a forceful statement that there should be nothing done to threaten the social gains the Afghan women had made since 2001.

India's then foreign minister, S.M. Krishna, tried to remind the international community in London about the central role of Pakistan in supporting the Taliban, "For Afghanistan's stabilisation it is essential for the neighbouring and regional countries to ensure that support, sustenance and sanctuaries for terrorist organisations is ended forthwith."

But there were few takers for India's arguments that the Afghan war had to be tackled by putting pressure on the Taliban through their main patron, Pakistan. Western governments faced growing demand at home to bring their troops home. The US policy took almost the opposite track: the US should increase its military and civilian aid commitments to Pakistan to bribe Islamabad into making the Taliban more amenable to a post-withdrawal Afghan political settlement.

In a June speech, India's Foreign Secretary Nirupama Rao stressed that security imperatives underlay India's development assistance in Afghanistan. She also laid out India's political vision of the country, in words that India was to repeat again and again in various fora. "The security of Afghanistan and what happens there impacts us…A stable and settled Afghanistan, where the rank and file of the Taliban has given up violence against the government, and the people cut all links with terrorism, subscribe to the values of the Afghan Constitution and its laws, and where development is the hard rationale, is what we seek and quest for."[15] But no one in the international community was listening.

As 2010 progressed, India's Afghan policy seemed to be increasingly marginalised. The US president publicly committed to a US withdrawal from Afghanistan that would begin in July 2011. At another International conference on Afghanistan in Istanbul, India was not even invited—at the insistence of Pakistan. Even Russia, a traditional Indian friend, assumed that Islamabad would rule the Kabul roost once the US withdrew and began making overtures to Pakistan because of its own security fears regarding the Taliban.

By the middle of 2010, New Delhi began to conclude that in the present circumstances perhaps a speedy US withdrawal from Afghanistan was perhaps in India's interest. This was partly driven by a sense that such a withdrawal was inevitable. India also came to the view that the Taliban of today was not quite the same as the pre-2001 Taliban. While hardly sympathetic to India, New Delhi concluded that the Afghan Taliban was more independent of Pakistan than most realised.

Most importantly, it was also concluded that the more drawn out the US process was, the more Washington would provide succour to the Pakistani military in the form of aid and political concessions. Between 2001 and 2008, the US had provided Pakistan US$ 11.8 billion worth of aid—80 per cent of which had gone to the military.[16] This was doubly bad because the Indian view was that the Pakistan military was at the root of not only the Taliban but, more worryingly in the long term, the weakening of secularism and civilian politics in Pakistan. In addition, a Pakistani military given injections of US money was more inclined to be obstructive about a peace process between India and Pakistan. The new head of the Pakistani military, General Ashfaq Parvez Kayani, had gone back on much that Musharraf had negotiated with India and it was believed that an expectation of a Pakistani geopolitical victory in Afghanistan was one of the reasons for his hard line.[17]

If the US wanted to leave, then it would be best for India if it were leave as soon as possible. India's past decade of gains in Afghanistan would be diluted, but even worse would be for India's gains against Pakistan—through dint of greater economic growth and Pakistan's reputation as a terrorist epicentre—to be lost as well.

However, there was another thread began to run through 2010. This was one of a Pakistan, sensing victory for its strategic goals in Afghanistan, beginning to overstep itself. In February 2010, the ISI and the US intelligence officials arrested Mullah Abdul Ghani Baradar, a Taliban leader who, it was determined, had begun secret talks with Karzai as part of an attempt to strike a peace agreement that was outside Islamabad's diktat. Barhanuddin Rabbani, Karzai's special envoy for peace talks, was assassinated in September, a death preceded by the murder of Karzai's brother, Wali.

Recommitment: 2011-12

Near the end of 2010, Obama made his first state visit to India. The US president was more inclined towards India than he had been at the beginning of his term. His attempts to seek an accommodation with China had led only to bruising humiliation. Pakistan had long been playing a double game in Afghanistan of giving passage to the US for supplies to its troops in Afghanistan, even while giving safe haven to the Taliban who were killing US troops. He had also developed a personal liking for Indian Prime Minister Manmohan Singh whose professorial style mimicked that of Obama's.

The joint statement they issued during the November visit marked the beginning of a bilateral strategic conversation between the two countries over Afghanistan. The statement said that 'the two sides committed to intensify consultation, cooperation and coordination to promote a stable, democratic, prosperous, and independent Afghanistan...They reiterated that success in Afghanistan and regional and global security require elimination of safe havens and infrastructure for terrorism and violent extremism in Afghanistan and Pakistan'.

India was reassured because of signals it was receiving that the US withdrawal would not necessarily be as drastic as it originally seemed. The original sense in New Delhi that Afghanistan was about to fall into Pakistan's lap once again, and that this would mean a resumption of the terror problem that India had faced before, were beginning to abate.

As it was, other events that year were to lead to the near collapse of the US-Pakistan relationship. The unprecedented degree of distrust between the two countries that was to arise would only strengthen US plans for a withdrawal that would keep Kabul independent of Islamabad.

In May 2011, a US special forces carried out a surprise attack on a house in Abbottabad, in the heart of Pakistani Punjab, and killed Al Qaeda leader and 9/11 mastermind Osama Bin Laden. Pakistan responded furiously at this humiliating violation of its security. But it could provide no ready explanation of how Bin Laden could have been hiding out in a high security zone surrounded by Pakistani military establishments without the help of someone senior in uniform. This had been preceded by other spats between the two countries. Among the more notable being the Raymond Davis incident when a US intelligence officer shot two ISI officers whom he thought were about to attack him.

Abbottabad reinforced a developing a US strategy of replacing the regular troops it was pulling out with a combination of armed drones and special forces. Nation building had long been abandoned. The more comprehensive counterterrorism-focussed policy was now visibly functioning.

The US withdrawal was going to happen, nonetheless. This had a number of consequences.

Karzai, who had become almost paranoid about the US's supposed unreliability as an ally, was pursuing an ever more independent policy in Afghanistan. This included trying to negotiate a power-sharing agreement with a portion of the Taliban. His idea was to find a political settlement that would allow him to survive a US withdrawal. He had even tried to work out a deal with Pakistan. But the demands made by Islamabad were so severe and humiliating that, to India's relief, the Afghan president had returned to a policy of trying to curb Pakistan's influence by splitting the Taliban. Karzai often expressed his suspicions about the US with Indian interlocutors (private conversation with Indian diplomats).

The so-called Arab Spring, a series of popular protests that had led to the fall of authoritarian rulers in Egypt and Tunisia, only fuelled Karzai's fears as he watched the US allow dictators who had been their surrogates for decades, like Hosni Mubarak, to fall from power.

A senior Indian foreign policy official noted in a closed door speech in New Delhi, "The shock [of Mubarak's fall] was greatest on those dependent on the US for their political survival like Karzai and on US allies like the Pakistani Army. Karzai's first reaction was to turn to Pakistan for support. Once again the Pakistanis overplayed their hand, killing his brother and Rabbani. And a worried Karzai now plays every card he can find, including a strategic partnership with India…"

After a year where India's Afghan position had been under mortal threat, 2011 saw the pendulum swing savagely in the opposite direction. The US withdrawal became increasingly a reconfiguration of military action. The US and Afghan distrust of Pakistan's intentions had increased dramatically. A sense that tighter criteria had to be set for any possible settlement with the Taliban was increasing. More countries were looking to India as a possible hedge for what might happen in a post-withdrawal Afghanistan.

The Bonn conference on Afghanistan saw the members lay down 'seven principles of reconciliation' as a compulsory element of international acceptance of any peace agreement. India played a constructive role at the conference even while a peeved Pakistan boycotted the talks.

At Bonn, India's Foreign Minister S.M. Krishna emphasised the new Indian line on Afghanistan that a post-withdrawal regime must be assured of a steady flow of billions of dollars in assistance. "We are clear that long-term international assistance to Afghanistan is not offered an expression of our collective munificence. It stems from our shared recognition that instability and radicalism in Afghanistan poses a threat to our common security," he said.

The new Indian buzzword on Afghanistan was 'Najibullah'. This was a reference to the last pro-Soviet Afghan leader to rule in Kabul. Though Najibullah had been declared dead on arrival when the last Soviet troops withdrew, he in fact held off the mujahedin for another three years thanks to a regular supply of Soviet money and arms. In fact, he survived longer than the Soviet Union did and his government fell only because he lost this lifeline.

Crudely, New Delhi came to see this as the model for a post-withdrawal Afghan regime. A continued US military presence of several thousand Special Forces and a fleet of armed drones, combined with several billion dollars of international aid, would allow Karzai or his successor to hold off the Taliban—and thus Pakistani influence—for many years to come.[17] India's policy, therefore, would be to try and ensure that these commitments were maintained. At a minimum, such a scenario would allow Kabul to negotiate an understanding with Pakistan on the future of Afghanistan from a position of equality.

Though the consequence would be a low-level war in Afghanistan that could go on for decades, India believed it was better than the original scenario of a return to Taliban regime in Kabul.

Also, the evidence of the past few years had been that the war in Afghanistan had begun undermining Islamabad's own security and making it more amenable towards India.

At least one branch of the Taliban, the Tehreek-e-Taliban, had turned its guns against Pakistan. The government's writ in the border areas with Afghanistan was decreasing. Pakistan had been forced to move some 1,50,000 troops from the Indian border to the west in an attempt to stabilise the areas adjoining Afghanistan. As a consequence, even General Kayani had concluded he could ill-afford a squabble with India at this point and had given the green signal for the peace process to go ahead with India.

Islamabad had, for example, granted most favoured nation status to India after a delay of decades. Kashmir was relatively quiet. With US military aid drying up, the Pakistani military would also be more inclined to caution.

Afghanistan was becoming Pakistan's quagmire, and this was providing India a degree of leverage it had not had since the years that just followed 9/11. The Afghanistan issue, in just over a decade, had come full circle for India. What has been striking, however, is that India has increasingly come to exploit its Afghan policy and events in that country to push forward its agenda regarding Pakistan. India, it can be argued, has had a policy that has been 'AfPak' from the very beginning.

Notes

1. Ahmed Rashid's definitive account *Taliban: Militant Islam, Oil and Fundamentalism in Central Asia*, 2nd edition, Yale University Press, 2010.
2. Background briefings by Foreign Minister Jaswant Singh to senior journalists all through 2001.
3. Pakistan on the Brink, Allen Lane, 2012" should read *"Pakistan on the Brink,* (London: Allen Lane, 2012).
4. In conversations the author had with US and Indian diplomats.
5. In private conversation the author had with US and Indian officials.
6. For details of the aid programme, see details of the aid programme can be found. http://www.mea.gov.in/Portal/ForeignRelation/afghanistan-aug-2012.pdf
7. Rashid, *Pakistan On the Brink*, p. 21.
8. On the back channel. http://ibnlive.in.com/news/exclusive-musharraf-on-missed-kashmir-deal/97374-2.html
9. For a detailed description of the US's helplessness over the Kabul embassy attack see David Sanger, *The Inheritance*, Broadway, 2010.
10. Bob Woodward, *Obama's Wars,* (New York: Simon & Schuster, 2011) p. 34
11. http://www.nytimes.com/2010/12/17/world/asia/17afghan.html?_r=2&hp
12. Woodward, Op. cit.
13. Ibid. 209.
14. (On Narayanan's warning, see http://www.ft.com/intl/cms/s/0/a545f3b0-f1f9-11dd-9678-0000779fd2ac.html; on Holbrooke. http://thecable.foreignpolicy.com/posts/2009/01/23/india_s_stealth_lobbying_against_holbrooke
15. http://www.ambinde.fr/speeches-and-statements/107-speech-by-foreign-secretary-on-afghanistan-india-pakistan-trialogue-organised-by-delhi-policy-group-13-june-2010
16. Rashid, *Pakistan on the Brink*, p. 71.
17. http://articles.timesofindia.indiatimes.com/2010-03-20/pakistan/28127179_1_pakistan-army-zardari-ashfaq-parvez-kayani
18. http://www.nytimes.com/2012/02/05/world/asia/us-plans-a-shift-to-elite-forces-in-afghanistan.html?pagewanted=all

6. Urban Vulnerabilities in 'Post-Conflict' Afghanistan

Arpita Basu Roy

Keywords: vulnerability, Afghanistan, transition, peace building, reconstruction, institution building, livelihood security, environment, management, governance

Introduction

Vulnerability has been defined as 'the exposure to contingencies and stress, and difficulties coping with them' and the term 'vulnerability' has been developed as a recognised conceptual framework and analytical approach to address marginality and poverty through means other than economic terms alone.[1] The paper proposes to discuss the trends and vulnerabilities in urban spaces in 'post-conflict' Afghanistan. The number of urban residents in Afghanistan in the post-2001 period has risen dramatically due to migration from the rural areas and repatriation from neighbouring lands, leaving the international donor community and the local government to increasingly look at ways to address the challenges of urban planning and poverty. Vulnerability has thus two sides—(1) an external side of risks, shocks and stress to which an individual or household is subject, and (2) an internal side which is defencelessness, meaning a lack of means to cope without damaging loss.[2] Afghanistan being a perfect case of a Situation of Chronic Conflict and Political Instability (SCCPIs) having generic features like weakened state institutions, strong parallel or non-formal economies, existence of, or high susceptibility to violence, forced displacement of people, the denial of basic human rights to sections of the community, lack of livelihoods and existence of serious poverty which produce specific vulnerabilities for the people is a perfect case to study vulnerabilities in post–conflict reconstruction situation. Vulnerability has become a recognised analytical approach in research and applications dealing with uncertainty and risks, especially in terms of livelihood security.[3]

Afghanistan's urban transition is precipitating a crisis in local governance. Against an analysis of peace building and post-conflict reconstruction, the paper would argue that Afghanistan's urban poor has little or no access to basic services and social infrastructure because of a result of limited resources, combined with the authorities' unwillingness and lack of capacity to serve effectively. It analyses situation in the different urban spaces in Afghanistan and shows that there are determinants that shape and differentiate the situations of the poor and the vulnerable. By interpreting the various vulnerabilities as human security threats, it shows how exclusion from basic services adversely affects the capacity of the urban poor to earn adequate income and acquire the necessary human assets to have quality of life. While lack of services has long been recognised as a major problem in urban Afghanistan, investments in safe water supply, sanitation, shelter and pollution-free environment have largely been insufficient. By highlighting such crises of urbanisation the paper, by way of conclusion, would argue for democratic representation and efficient urban management.

Peace building in 'Post–conflict' spaces
The term peace building is broadly used and is associated with activities that go beyond crisis intervention such as longer-term development, and building of governance structures and institutions. The general understanding of the peace building enterprise is largely influenced by the former UN Secretary-General Boutros Boutros-Ghali's vision and direction for peace

building in his 1992 document *An Agenda for Peace*.⁴ According to this UN document, peace building consists of a wide range of activities associated with capacity building, <u>reconciliation</u>, and societal <u>transformation</u>.⁵ Experiences in various parts of the world in the mid-1990s have shown that sustained peace based on political and military stabilisation is not sufficient to end a protracted conflict based on ethnic, religious, and other primordially fuelled rivalries, in the absence of a long-term perspective of structural transformation.⁶ Post-conflict peace building is connected to peacekeeping, and often involves demobilisation and reintegration programmes, as well as immediate reconstruction needs.⁷ Various transformation techniques aim to move parties away from confrontation and violence, and guide them towards political and economic participation, peaceful relationships, and social harmony.⁸ Such transformation is most crucial in urban spaces where reconstruction needs are maximum.

> "Peace building should essentially mean a wide range of sequential activities, proceeding from cease-fire and refugee-resettlement to the establishment of a new government and economic reconstruction.⁹ Peace building in post-settlement phase entails both short-term and long-term frameworks. In the absence of local administrative structures, essential government functions are restored by international administrators or peacekeeping forces. According to Ho-Wong Jeong, the goals of peace building will ultimately be achieved by reconstruction and reconciliation that are geared not only towards changing behaviour and perceptions but also towards social and institutional structures that can be mobilized to prevent future conflict.¹⁰ The UN is committed to peace building in the world because of a conviction to achieve the great objective of the charter i.e. to maintain international peace and security, of securing justice and human rights and of promoting, in the words of the Charter, "Social progress and better standards of life in larger freedom."¹¹

Development cannot be easily disentangled from democracy and security.[12] 'Post-conflict reconstruction' supports the transition from conflict to peace in an affected country through the rebuilding of the socioeconomic framework of the society. Wars often cause huge impacts such as death and injury to much of the population, massive displacement of people as refugees and Internally Displaced Persons (IDPs), widespread destruction of properties, poor institutional capacity and vulnerability to disease and crime.[13] Further, conflicts greatly reduce the security, prevent access to production facilities and erode the social capital.[14] In this context the rebuilding of war torn urban spaces of a conflict-zone becomes very crucial.

The Afghan Context

> In societies like Afghanistan, where conflict has been controlled to a certain degree, 'peace building' also involves a complex process of negotiations, new challenges and opportunities for social transformation particularly when the international community is an unwieldy entity with no single centre and lots of contradiction. It comprises the major world powers, with the United States as the dominant agent in some situations and as a reluctant participant in others. In Afghanistan, for instance, the US wants to have complete control over war operations but did not involve itself with peacekeeping activities like social empowerment, development or political transition. Meanwhile, the multilateral organisations that are bound by their mandates to play the dominant role in peacekeeping and state reconstruction, like the United Nations, remained the weakest and most divided of all.[15]

In Afghanistan, with the international coalition and US-backed Afghan insurgents removing the *Taliban* from power, there has been a struggle to establish a centralised and legitimate democratic government. The blueprint of nation-building in Afghanistan which has been laid down by the Bonn Agreement of 2001 faced challenges of political, economic and social dimensions. Certain challenges had been identified by the World Bank,[16] which included the widespread destruction of infrastructure; low social indicators; prevalence of drugs and arms; delicate, uncertain and factionalised politics; legacy of a three-year drought and extremely weak administrative capacity. The poor infrastructure of the country, the continuing drought, the high number of Internally Displaced Persons and refugees in neighbouring countries, the gender inequality—all added to the enormity of the transitional challenge. The unsettled military and political environment along with the competing regional and international interests further threatens to influence the process and outcome.[17]

War-torn countries, anyway, are characterised by death and injuries of much of the people, massive displacement of people as refugees and Internally Displaced Persons (IDPs), widespread destruction of properties, poor institutional capacities and vulnerability to disease and crimes. In a context where conflict was controlled to a large extent, we find a large number of refugees and internally displaced settling in urban spaces. There is worldwide boom in urbanisation and Afghanistan is no exception. Out of the total settled population of Afghanistan of 2,55,00,100, the total urban settled population is 60,74,200 with total settled population of Kabul Province being 33,09,400.[18] Urban dwellers in the country are about 25 per cent of the total population. Most cities are currently experiencing a steady influx of returned refugees and internally displaced persons (IDPs), and by 2015, the number of urban residents in Afghanistan is expected to double, growing at a rate twice as high as the average growth rate in the rural areas.

Vulnerabilities in Urban Afghanistan
The term vulnerability started being used in the late 1980s, after

researchers and practitioners expressed discomfort in defining marginality and poverty solely through economic terms. Since then, vulnerability has become a recognised conceptual framework and analytical approach in research and applications dealing with uncertainty and risks, especially in terms of livelihood security. In practical terms, the concept is predominant in guiding actions taken by government and Non-governmental Organisations (NGOs) trying to identify and target recipients of their services. This study involved many questions that need first hand information, to be collected from the study universe. In other words, some stakeholders were approached in Kabul for their perspective on the ground realities of the study universe. Ideally, primary information should be collected by formulating missions to the area of study. The proposed study universe which are the urban spaces of Afghanistan, not being suitable for application of such methodological rigour primary data has been collected from reliable agencies working and collecting data from the study universe. However the authors' various trip to the study universe helped her develop some perspectives on Kabul.

In Afghanistan, projected annual changes in 'percentage urban' (1.98-2.34 per cent for Afghanistan) are above regional averages (1.16-1.42 per cent for Asia),[19] according to a study conducted in 2005.[20] This development is put down to three trends: self-generated growth (urban natural increase, i.e. urban births exceeding urban deaths.); net in-migration (Urban in-migration exceeding urban out-migration) fuelled by economic scarcity, unemployment, and environmental hazards (mainly droughts) in rural areas, as well as refugee return flows (both assisted and spontaneous). Respondents from the United Nations High Commissioner for Refugees (UNHCR) as well as international agencies and NGOs dealing with refugees and IDPs, such as the International Organization for Migration (IOM), emphasised that refugees and IDPs returned to their villages of origin. However, the qualitative evidence suggests that due to a lack of livelihood and other opportunities in the countryside, a significant number of assisted returnees immediately left the countryside for the city. This implies that Afghanistan's urban population may be underestimated, constituting an important area of further research. In another study conducted by AREU on Kabul, Jalalabad, and Herat, what is visible is the stark similarity in the vulnerabilities of the urban poor.[21] The economy can be described as what is best known as 'coping economies' characterised by a widespread struggle for survival in a high–risk environment. In such situations people are often found facing depleting asset bases often rely on the employment of child labour, leading to long-term negative effects on health-status and education.[22]

Also within the context of post conflict reconstruction, housing reconstruction plays an important role in establishing the country's development and peace. Post conflict reconstruction requires repair and reconstruction of housing, social and economic infrastructure of conflict affected countries. Reintegration of displaced people can lead the country towards development and then peace as well. However, most of the housing projects are not appropriate for the beneficiaries' needs and socio-economic conditions. A sustainable housing must be appropriate to the needs of the family, suitable to the local environment and located in an area where there is employment and where services are adequate to the needs of the occupants. Informal settlements now account for the larger part of houses in Afghanistan's urban centres. Housing shortages, high rents, diminished housing stock, and the influx of returnees, internally displaced people and expatriate development workers all exacerbate the problem. The absence of an effective and coherent land management system in growing urban centres has provided opportunities for illicit dealings, whether by politicians, government officials, private militias, or unscrupulous land developers.[23]

The capital of Afghanistan, Kabul, has suffered immensely from war and destruction, leaving large parts of the city in a deplorable condition. Moreover, the high influx of refugee returnees since 2001 has put additional pressure on an already overloaded service infrastructure and the limited job market. Migrants from other parts of the country have also flocked into the city, seeking employment, public services, and/or agency assistance in the wake of the opportunities offered by the new government and by the many international organisations involved in security and reconstruction activities who have established offices there since December 2001. Kabul's current population is therefore quite heterogeneous, in contrast to most of Afghanistan's more homogeneous rural communities. Much of Kabul's physical infrastructure has been destroyed following decades of conflict and lack of maintenance. This has created housing shortages and service delivery backlogs resulting in, for example, a lack of clean water supply and urban traffic congestion. There is a shortage of low income housing.[24] This has encouraged the spread of informal, or squatter, settlements throughout Kabul. It is estimated that as many as half of the city's population live in squatter settlements. Moreover, the high number of international organisations in Kabul also has quite adverse effects on urban livelihoods, as due to their presence, prices in the city have increased significantly. Ecologically, life in Kabul poses the additional problem of quite harsh winters.

The citizens of Kabul are faced with sharp increase in land prices and rents, as aid, commercial, military and other organisations with international currency operating funds move into Kabul. Land speculation has led to a proliferation of high rise, high rent buildings owned by Afghan merchants and powerbrokers in sharp contrast to the city's widespread squatter settlements symbolic of the wealth disparities (and tensions) in the city. Often these new buildings are not in compliance with extant municipal zoning or building codes.

There are, however, currently no effective mechanisms for the enforcement of these regulations. There are significant land tenure issues, including property disputes arising from war and regime changes.

The city of Jalalabad is the urban centre of eastern Nangarhar Province located in the junction of Kabul and Kunar rivers. Population figures are somewhat variable, ranging from about 1,81,000 to 5,00,000. There is wide seasonal fluctuation in population numbers, with people moving in to temporarily escape the winter months in Kabul. In addition, the city's proximity to Pakistan results in patterns of seasonal migration, mostly in search of work abroad. There is a significant proportion of IDPs living in Jalalabad or in camps very close to the city, many of whom sought refuge in the years of war and decided to stay rather than return to their native places. Jalalabad's closeness to the border of Pakistan makes the city an important trading centre for all kinds of goods and foodstuffs. Urban vulnerability seems to be present largely in the form of food insecurity for many households, though the overall situation has been judged more favourable than in Kabul. Living conditions for the poor and vulnerable in squatter settlements and IDP camps are characterised by widespread lack of basic services like water and electricity. Livelihood strategies try to take advantage of job opportunities in Pakistan, but even more so from efforts in finding access to employment in the agricultural wage labour sector of Nangarhar District.

The city of Herat is located in western Afghanistan in close proximity to Iran and Turkmenistan. Quite similar to Jalalabad in the east, its location makes Herat an important commercial centre with significant trade relations to neighbouring countries. The city, with its very rich and ancient cultural heritage, has an estimated population of 2,49,000.[25] Unregulated customs duties from border traffic and a high trade volume contribute to the city's development and relative wealth. As such, a well-maintained infrastructure in Herat gives the impression of prosperity, especially when compared with other towns in Afghanistan. In spite of this, urban poverty is highly visible, especially in the numerous squatter settlements on the outskirts of town. Additionally, the city has attracted a large number of migrants from drought-affected rural areas, as well as returned refugees from Iran. This has put pressure on an already limited job market and resulted in a decrease of the price of labour and falling daily wages. As such, there is a wide difference in living standards in Herat, with a huge number of inhabitants able to take advantage of a relatively stable political situation and the position of the town on major trade routes. Yet living conditions of the urban poor and vulnerable in Herat are similar to those in Kabul or Jalalabad. Malnutrition has been observed, squatter settlements are widespread, insecure casual and daily labour function as sources of income and an overall decline in entitlements is abundant. However, Herat's proximity to Iran also provides opportunities. Labour migration of male household members is widespread and remittances from abroad are often the most important means for managing livelihoods.

Kandahar or Qandahar is the second largest city and one of the most culturally significant cities of the Pashtuns in Afghanistan, with a population of about 5,12,200 as of 2011. Kandahar has been the Pashtuns' traditional seat of power for hundreds of years. It is a major trading centre for sheep, wool, cotton, silk, felt, food grains, fresh and dried fruit, and tobacco. The region produces fine fruits, especially pomegranates and grapes, and the city has plants for canning, drying, and packing fruit. The region around Kandahar is one of the oldest known human settlements.[26] Kandahar is Afghanistan's fast-growing southern urban hub of commerce. The area has been devastated through heavy fighting—not only during the Soviet period but also when the Americans attacked the Taliban in 2001—and many walls and homes were in ruins. This has not inhibited the return of many refugees and IDPs, however, who are living in their small compounds throughout the area along with other newly arrived squatters who seek shelter in the many destroyed structures and bunkers.

Poor urban dwellers struggle to make ends meet, with income used primarily for food, house reconstruction and costly medical care. Sending children to school calls for additional direct costs for school supplies (notebooks, pens, pencils, books), uniforms, and in some cases, transportation (like rickshaws utilised especially for girls)—an ongoing commitment on the part of parents and the household in general.[27] The amount spent on these direct costs varied considerably according to the number of children in the household enrolled in school. Under-nutrition is especially common among women and children in the poorer households. and in the case of infants, this is often accompanied by chronic diarrhoea. Drug addiction was a problem in some households, sometimes resulting in domestic violence. The following complicated example from a poor nuclear unit illustrates the links between economic problems, stress, conflict between spouses, costly health care and selling of household assets in the poorer households, adult females were also active in home-based income generation, which included sewing (four women) and embroidering (three women) for cash, along with selling eggs (one old woman). In a report published in 2005 a number of households had sold some of their physical assets—both productive and non-productive—in recent years.[28]

Stefan Schutte's study shows that for the urban context, coping economies tend to be characterised by widespread unemployment, a subsequent loss of income, insecure and expensive housing, food insecurity, and lack of long-term investment and tenure rights. Involvement in the urban coping economies of Afghanistan poses rather similar conditions for the poor and vulnerable, and these tend to be more encompassing than the differences between each city. However, there are also differences between the groups under study, with gender and physical health being important markers.

Human Security Threats in Urban Spaces

Livelihood Security

There are several risks to livelihood security in urban Afghanistan. There are risks of unemployment, loss of income and indebtedness. Urban labour markets in Afghanistan are generally highly diversified, but for the unskilled and less literate labour force, access to opportunities is usually limited to the heterogeneous sector of informal employment. Job opportunities for unskilled persons are unreliable, irregular and subject to high seasonal variance. Most people have huge difficulties in finding constant and secure sources of income, which keeps their available cash at an erratic and low level. Naturally, common forms of coping with unemployment and irregularities of income are the employment of child labour and establishing access to credit. The former often leads to a depletion of educational levels, the latter to indebtedness. Unfortunately, several households are entrapped in a vicious cycle of having to decide between either sending their kids to school to learn or in the streets to make money, leaving very limited space for children to negotiate between school and work. Educated individuals also have difficulties finding employment in present day Afghanistan. Their participation in cash for work activities, like picking garbage and digging ditches, is perceived as very humiliating and reveals a certain degree of despair among the educated urban population. Generally, employment opportunities for women are very limited. A kind of 'cultural vulnerability' leaves little space for them. With their mobility harshly restricted, some women may manage to find work as servants, cleaning staff, or carpet weavers, but more choices hardly exist. People with less competitive power, such as the elderly, people with disabilities and other health problems are also particularly susceptible to loss of income and indebtedness.

Food Insecurity

The question of food security is not inseparable from loss of income, because in urban areas sufficient nourishment depends on whether a household can afford to buy enough food. In the absence of subsistence production, levels of cash income, in combination with fluctuating food prices, are the most important factors influencing household supplies. However, the ample evidence of existing malnutrition. In the context of urban food security it is the ability of an individual or household to render its endowments into effective command over food, be it via direct access or exchange relations, through mobilising resources out of social networks, through state support or through humanitarian assistance. The urban poor and vulnerable are not capable of making sufficient use of their asset base to obtain command over food, leading to the observed problems of malnutrition and hidden hunger. In the words of Drèze and Sen:

> "The life of a person can be seen as a sequence of things the person does, or states of being he or she achieves ... 'Capability' refers to the alternative combinations of functionings from which a person can choose. Thus, the notion of capability is essentially one of freedom — the range of options a person has in deciding what kind of a life to lead ... poverty is, thus, ultimately a matter of capability deprivation."[29]

Employment of child labour, finding access to loans, begging and mobilising social resources are the most common strategies utilised in all three cities. Begging takes different forms. It is generally perceived as a humiliating practice, and often women and children rely upon begging as a last resort. Interestingly, in surveys conducted in the three cities—Kabul, Jalalabad, and Herat—women emerged as great managers of social relations and in spite of mobility restrictions, women are important managers of social relations, on which they can rely for support infrequently in case of need.

These relations include not only shopkeepers, but also neighbours, extended family or friends. Bigger households may face difficulties in securing sufficient food intake for all, especially when there is a limited number of productively working household members, and thus, a high dependency rate. Household composition in terms of gender and health also influence income opportunities and thus levels of food security. Households headed by women, people with disabilities or elderly persons seem to be explicitly exposed to the risk of food insecurity. Functioning social networks have the potential capacity to act as critical safety nets and to help reduce food insecurity.

Health Security
There are clear consequences of what food and livelihood insecurity can have on health. Loss of income and food insecurity both have negative consequences on physical and mental well-being and they compound into one another. A lack of income prevents investing in health care, which in turn may lead to illness. Poor health of the main breadwinner of a household may result in further income loss and may put livelihoods of all members of a household at risk. Facilities for health care are present in all three cities studied, though, as the ACF survey states, overall quality of public health services in Kabul is very poor and ineffective. Apart from that, access is limited, as costs of treatment usually surpass the financial capacities of the poor and vulnerable, or facilities are located far away from the vulnerable neighbourhoods. Alternative, good quality health care in private clinics is inaccessible to the poor, as consultation fees may already exceed the daily income realised through casual labour. Without basic resources in place, many households do not attempt to seek professional medical treatment. It is more likely that people approach pharmacies directly and seek advice to their problems in order to avoid expensive prescription

fees of clinics or doctors. Obtaining loans for treatment, reducing the labour force to provide constant care for household members in need and trying to mobilise social relations for support are certainly the most important coping strategies. Poor housing, lack of sanitary facilities, defective water supply or inadequate waste and sewage disposal are some of the reasons for susceptibility to health risks. Young children and adolescents can be critically affected by insufficient nutritional intake, and combined with hard work and little recreational time, are vulnerable to deteriorating health. War victims, the disabled and women in general have a certain disposition to experience mental health problems, caused by overall worrying about household situations, problems of physical health or humiliating experiences in the past.

Environmental Security
The legacy of conflict that has plagued Afghanistan and its people for nearly 30 years has damaged not only the country's society and institutions, but also its environment. Environmental degradation, and poor access to clean and safe drinking water and sanitation, is major environmental security threat to people. The lack of available energy services correlates closely with many poverty indicators, while urban dwellers are exposed to many toxic and carcinogenic air pollutants.[30] The main impacts are the depletion and overuse of important resources (forests, biodiversity, water), which exacerbates the stressful socio-economic conditions and the impact of natural hazards; reduced access to natural resources; erosion of the rule of law; collapse of traditional governance systems and processes; pollution with toxic rocket fuel, spilled oil and land mines, making essential land and pastures unsafe to use.[31] Moreover, surface and groundwater scarcity and contamination, massive and ongoing deforestation, desertification of important wetlands, soil erosion, air pollution, and depleted wildlife populations.

Nationwide, the majority of Afghan households do not have access to safe drinking water. Because of unsafe sanitary facilities, water contamination is a major issue in Afghanistan, including capital Kabul. Many water sources are contaminated with harmful bacteria, such as E. Coli, which sickens and kills many people, especially children and the elderly. Valuable water resources are polluted as a result of the disposal of industrial and domestic liquid wastes. In addition, the prolonged lack of water and the rapid disappearance of half of the country's forest and woodland cover turned thousands of people into environmental refugees. This has led to increased population pressure on over-burdened urban areas and could generate new small-scale conflicts over access to scarce resources. National capacity to address these problems is severely limited as a result of the collapse of local and national forms of governance and resource management.[32] In fact the most serious issue in Afghanistan is the long-term environmental degradation caused, in part, by a complete collapse of local and national forms of governance.[33] Due to over-population in many urban areas and the high concentration of pollution sources such as cars and industries, the residents suffer from severe air pollution, poorly organised collection and disposal of waste, lack of sanitation and access to safe drinking water. There is also a shortage of green open spaces.[34] Climate change, the resulting melting of mountain glaciers, severe droughts and poor management of water resources are also threatening water security.[35] Water is key to the health and well-being of people, and essential to maintaining agricultural productivity which is at the heart of the Afghan economy.[36] Many of the country's wetlands are completely dry and no longer support wildlife populations or provide agricultural inputs. For example, UNEP found that over 99 per cent of the Sistan wetland, a critically important haven for waterfowl was completely dry.

Table 1: Forms, Sources and determinants of urban vulnerability

Form of Vulnerability	Vulnerability to Income Failure	Vulnerability to Food Insecurity	Vulnerability to bad health	Vulnerability to social exclusion and disempowerment
Source of Vulnerability	Exposure to an unreliable and erratic labour market	Capability Deprivation Decline of entitlements	Poor living and working conditions	Powerlessness and marginalisation
Determinants of Vulnerability	Quality of health Levels of Education Household Composition Diversification of Income Sources	Vagaries of market forces Income Levels	Quality of Housing Income Levels Access to Health Care Access to Clean Water and Sanitation	Quality of intra-and inter-household relations Time and resources available to keep up social relations Social affiliation Membership in social networks

Source: Urban Vulnerability in Afghanistan: Case Studies from three cities, AREU, May 2004

Conclusion: Managing the Cities

Afghanistan's urban poor suffers as a result of limited resources, and has inadequate access to basic services and social infrastructure. There are determinants that shape and differentiate the situations of the poor and the vulnerable. Some households manage to achieve longer-term wellbeing while others endure perpetual poverty. Further, urban vulnerability is not necessarily linked to informal settlements, which often enjoy relatively good access to services and security of tenure due to the backing of powerful patrons. Exclusion from basic services adversely affects the capacity of the urban poor to earn adequate income and acquire the necessary human assets to have quality of life. While lack of services has long been recognised as a major problem in urban Afghanistan, investments in safe water supply, sanitation, shelter, and pollution-free environment have largely been insufficient for democratic representation and grassroots governance. Problems are further aggravated as it combines the authorities' unwillingness and lack of capacity to serve effectively.

Diligent management and inclusive governance is essential in 'post-conflict' Afghanistan. The fast-growing and vibrant cities of Afghanistan, which host roughly 25 per cent of the country's population, pose particular development problems but also carry significant potential for advancing social and economic well-being if they are diligently managed and inclusively governed. Urban governance needs more coordinated approach. Both require flexible approaches as well as enhanced cooperation between government departments as well as between those departments and city residents. This in turn entails a more collaborative and communicative approach to planning and management, both at the city and sub-city levels. Clearly, this constitutes a challenge, as many current urban planners are wedded to existing and familiar approaches and practices. Further, there are few young professionals coming into the system who have capacity in new methodologies, systems, and equipment. Yet, Afghanistan is blessed with a wealth of well-trained Afghan returnees who represent an opportunity for the modernisation of urban planning, management, and practice.

Urban management happens to be one of the twelve pillars of the National Development Plan of the Islamic Republic of Afghanistan. Increasingly the Afghan government is turning its attention to urban reconstruction and development and donors are beginning to respond to these challenges in a far more concerted manner. A critical focus is on the supply of infrastructure. Although this is crucial, unless urban management is effective and governance systems are sound, investments in physical development will not be sustainable or evenly spread. To this end, it is important that clarity is achieved over the functional responsibilities of different levels of government and government departments.

Notes
1. Chambers, R. "Vulnerability, coping and policy." *IDS Bulletin*, 20 (1989)., pp. 1-7.
2. Ibid.
3. Stefan Schutte, *Urban Vulnerability in Afghanistan: Case Studies from Three Cities*, Afghan Research and Evaluation Unit (AREU), Working Paper Series, Kabul, May 2004.
4. *An Agenda for Peace, Preventive Diplomacy, and Peacekeeping*, Report of the Secretary-General pursuant to the statement adopted by the Summit Meeting of the Security Council on January 31, 1992, A/47/277 - S/24111, June 17, 1992.
5. Boutros-Ghali, *An Agenda for Peace*, United Nations, New York, 1995.
6. The Peace building experiences from Somalia, Liberia, Haiti, and Bosnia-Herzegovina reflect the same.
7. Michael Doyle and Nicholas Sambanis, "Building Peace: Challenges and Strategies After Civil War," The World Bank Group, http://www.worldbank.org/research/conflict/papers/building.pdf, p. 3.
8. Ibid.
9. Ho-Won Jeong, *Peace building in Post Conflict Societies: Strategy and Process*, [New Delhi: Viva Books Private Limited (first Indian reprint, Copyright Lynne Rienner publishers), 2006], p. 1.
10. Ibid. p.12-13.
11. "Preamble," Charter of the United Nations.
12. Ho-Won Jeong, n. 9.
13. FAO, 2005.
14. World Bank, 1998.
15. Marina Ottaway, *Op. Cit.*, p. 20.
16. Alastair Mckechnie, Country Director: Afghanistan, *Reconstruction of Afghanistan: A World Bank Perspective*, Presentation Delivered to OECD-Development Assistance Committee, May 02, 2002.
17. Sultan Barakat, "Setting the Scene for Afghanistan's Reconstruction: the Challenges and Critical Dilemmas," *Third World Quarterly*, Vol. 23, No. 5, October 2002, pp. 801-816.
18. *Population Estimation 2012-13*, Central Statistics Organisation, Islamic

Republic of Afghanistan, http://cso.gov.af/en/page/6449 (Accessed on June 26, 2012).
19. UNDESA (United Nations Department of Economic and Social Affairs). *World Urbanisation Prospects: The 2003 Revision, Population Division 1.* (New York: UN, 2004).
20. Jo Beall and Daniel Esser, *Shaping Urban Futures: Challenges to Governing and Managing Afghan Cities,* Afghanistan Research and Evaluation Unit, Issues Paper Series, Kabul, March 2005.
21. Stefan Schutte, *Urban Vulnerability in Afghanistan: Case Studies from Three Cities,* AREU Working Paper Series, May 2004, p. 9.
22. A. Pain, and J Goodhand, *Afghanistan: Current Employment and Socio-economic Situation and Prospects.* In Focus Programmeme on Crisis Response and Reconstruction, Working Paper 8, (Geneva: ILO, 2002).
23. Jo Beall and Daniel Esser, *Shaping Urban Futures: Challenges to Governing and Managing Afghan Cities,* Afghanistan Research and Evaluation Unit, Issues Paper Series, March 2005.
24. Stefan Schutte, op cit.
25. Central Statistics Office (CSO), *Afghanistan Statistical Yearbook*, Issue No. 24, Kabul, 2003.
26. Alexander the Great had laid-out the foundation of what is now Old Kandahar in the 4th century BC. Since the 1978 Marxist revolution, the city has been a magnet for groups such as the Pakistan-based Haqqani network, Quetta Shura, Hezbi Islami, al-Qaida and other terrorist groups, many of which are believed to receive support from Pakistan's ISI spy network. From late 1994 to 2001, it served as the capital of the Taliban government until they were toppled by US-led NATO forces during Operation Enduring Freedom in late 2001 and replaced by the current government of President Hamid Karzai.
27. Pamela Hunte, *Household Decision-making and School Enrollment in Afghanistan, Case Study 4: District 2, Kandahar City,* AREU, Kabul, 2005.
28. One unit had sold its embroidery machine, dishes and jewellery in order to rebuild its war destroyed house; another family sold its wooden wheelbarrow (from which it used to sell things) and its dishes in order to pay off an old outstanding debt.
29. J. Drèze and A Sen, *India: Economic Development and Social Opportunity*, (Oxford/New York: Oxford University Press, 1995).
30. United Nations Environment Programmeme (UNEP), *From Conflict to Peacebuilding: The Role of Natural Resources and the Environment*, 2009.
31. Ibid.
32. *Afghanistan's Environmental Recovery: A Post-conflict Plan for People and their Natural Resources*, UNEP, August 2006.

33. Pekka Havisto, 'Introduction', *Afghanistan: Post Conflict Environmental Assessment*, UNEP, 2003.
34. United Nations Environment Programme, *From Conflict to Peace building: The Role of Natural Resources and the Environment*, 2009, p. 5.
35. Ibid, p. 11.
36. The first State of Environment (SOE) Report for Afghanistan, produced by the National Environmental Protection Agency (NEPA) with assistance from the United Nations Environment Programmeme (UNEP), point out that both surface and groundwater resources have been severely affected by the drought, as well as by uncoordinated and unmanaged extraction. It has been pointed out that in many cases, deep wells have been drilled without considering the long-term impacts on regional groundwater resources, including traditional *karez* systems (underground water canals). Water resources across the country are also threatened by contamination from waste dumps, chemicals and open sewers.

7. PASHTUNWALI AND ITS IMPACT ON INSURGENCY & RECONCILIATION EFFORTS IN AFGHANISTAN

Anwesha Ghosh

Introduction

The disintegration of the Safavid Empire to the West, of Mughal rule to the east, and continuing struggles among feudal rulers in Central Asia to the north provided opportunities for the Pashtun tribes to unite and lay foundation of an independent state in Afghanistan in the 18th centutry. Creation of such a state was in the best interest of Pashtun feudal landlords and clerics who could avert paying heavy taxes to the Persian and Mughal overlord. Since the establishment of modern Afghanistan in the 18th century by Ahmad Shah Abdali, a member of Sadozai Pashtun tribe of Kandahar, the tribes have played significant role in establishing and deposing different Afghan rulers. Tribal structures have especially played important role in respect to governance and security in areas where the central government could develop minimal reach over the years. The *'qawm'* had a dual effect in Afghanistan's history— on the one hand, it has prevented the central government from modernising the state structure; on the other hand, it has provided the crucial 'social capital' for the resilience of Afghan society to external shocks such as war, drought and failed Governance.[1] For the last 30 years or even more tribal structure or locally established *Shouras* have been only source of social justice in most part of Afghanistan.

Several value systems are competing with each other in Afghanistan presently, the understanding of the Pashtuns (their culture and traditional values) is often overshadowed by the Taliban and their fundamentalist rendition of Islam. This perspective handicaps the recognition of certain cultural values and rules of behaviour which have been determining the way of life for many Pashtuns. The Pashtuns, constituting approximately 38 to 42 per cent of the total population of Afghanistan (which makes them the single largest ethnic group), have been called "the most tribalised group of people in the world."[2] There are, however, some disputes among scholars and observers as to the importance of tribal system, especially in the post 2001 scenario, when the attempts of Interim Government set up after the Bonn Conference and the subsequent regime of President Hamid Karzai tried to set up a modern democratic polity in Afghanistan. This paper would try to bring back into the discourse the factor of *Pashtunwali*—a system of values and rules of behaviour, which for a rather long time before (and after) the rise of Taliban has been an integral feature of the Pashtun people. The paper means to explore its significance in the present-day. Even today, it has arguably a substantial hold among the Pashtun majority provinces of Afghanistan and tribal areas on the Pakistani side of the Durrand Line. This paper would attempt to examine if and how it has played or can play a role in the Afghan insurgency, as also the reconciliation efforts in contemporary Afghanistan.

Background of the Pashtun Tribal System
In Pashto language, most of these values and rules of behaviour are summarised under the word '*Pashtunwali*' or '*Pakhtunwali*', which can be understood as the 'way of the Pashtuns'.[3] Afghanistan and Pakistan have shared sensitive relations since inception and the controversies date back to the establishment of the Durand Line

in 1893 dividing Pashtun and Baloch tribes living in Afghanistan from those living in what later became Pakistan. The border region therefore could not be brought under control of any particular Government. FATA's seven tribal agencies—Khyber, Khurram, Orakzai, Mohamand, Bajaur and North and South Waziristan—are populated by just over three million tribesmen, adding to the twenty-eight million Pashtuns who live in Pakistan and the fifteen million in Afghanistan. The tribes on both sides of the border intermarry, trade, feud and celebrate with one another and adhere to Pashtunwali, the tribal code of honour and behaviour.[4]

Among Pashtun tribes, these values and rules of behaviour have been transmitted orally for centuries, but as late as the 1950s, some Afghan men of letters became more and more interested in Pashtunwali when searching for the guiding principles for a modern Afghan nation. After that Afghan scholars started studying Pashtunwali from a folkloric point of view. Thus written accounts on the subject appeared, offering a view from inside the culture of the Pashtuns. Though they serve as important guiding principles for behaviour, yet, ideals do not always measure up to reality. The rules of conduct of Pashtunwali follow the dichotomy of honour and shame.[5] Behaviour, accordingly, is guided by the question as to how it is assessed in the eyes of others according to common understanding of honour and shame. A person who embodies almost all of the values and rules of behaviour of Pashtunwali and who leaves no doubt that he does his utmost to abide by them is respectfully called *Ghairatman*—he represents the ideal Pashtun.[6] The concept of *ghairat* is probably the most complex tenet of Pashtunwali. The word means—(1) Dignity, self-esteem, pride, ambition; (2) Zeal, eagerness, passions; (3) Bravery, courage, audacity; (4) Indignation, anger; and (5) Modesty.[7] Thus, the concept of *ghairat* pools almost all values and rules of behaviour of the code of honour of the Pashtuns.

Evolution of the term Pashtunwali

The concept of Pashtunwali is ethno-centric because it is grounded on the idea that the Pashtuns are distinct from other ethnic groups not only because of their language, culture, history but due to their behaviour as well. The ideal of the way of life of the Pashtuns is sometimes confused with ethnic stereotype, but neither the ideal nor the stereotype corresponds to actual behaviour.[8] Though similar customs, values and norms can be found among other ethnic groups yet Pashtuns have evolved these values into a strong set of rules to a higher degree in comparison to other ethnic groups in the region.

It is said that during the relatively peaceful reign of King Zahir Shah (1933-73), if a crime was committed in even remotest part of districts of among tribal boundaries, the local elders were obliged to hand over the perpetrators to the government. This was despite the fact that even in those years, the government machinery was weak.[9] When British officials took notice of this norm in the 19th century, they became interested from administrative and military standpoints and their main focus went to customary law and blood revenge. From the account of East India Company officer, Montstuart Elphinstone, who visited Durrani winter residence in Peshawar in 1809, described Pashtunwali in his report as a 'rude system of customary law'.[10] Within Pashtun society the values, norms and rules of Pashtunwali have been orally transmitted for centuries, although as early as the 17th century, the Pashtun poet Khushhal Khan Khattak (1613-89) wrote a book in Pashto prose that can be seen as the first attempt to define rules of behaviour for Pashtuns, though the term 'Pashtunwali' did not occur in his book *Dastarnama*.[11] In modern time, the first written accounts on the subject appeared in 1950s, this time the authors were men of letters who followed the *Wesh Zalmiyan* Movement and other groups of intellectual enlightenment.[12] In their publication they popularized the values of Pashtunwali as educational maxims for a modern Afghan nation.

Nomadic Background of Pashtuns: Implications for *Pashtunwali*

Emergence of such norms of Pashtunwali was deep rooted in the social history of Pashtuns. The culture of honour can be identified with nomadic people who do not resort to Government for law enforcement when they traverse geographically in search of habitable pastures, and carry their most valuable property with them. Today, most Pashtuns live in rural areas and are engaged in agriculture. In nomadic societies private ownership of pasture land was unknown even though particular groups having a claim on a particular piece of land at a particular season of the year was in practice. However such claims were group claims and not individual. Group property of similar kind continued to exist with regard to pastures, threshing floors or woodlands.

Furthermore, it must be remembered that the Afghan state originally emerged from a Pashtun tribal confederacy. When Ahmed Shah Durrani was enthroned in 1747 as the king of Afghanistan, he was chosen by a group of Pashtun and Baluch tribal leaders. He could rely on the military and political strength of their tribes, which supported him as long as he did not offend their feelings and interest.[13] Same was the case with all his successors within the royal dynasties, all of them self-evidently were Pashtuns. Pashtun tribes provided political and military foundation to these dynasties and in return enjoyed numerous privileges which other ethnic groups didn't. Only the Baluch tribes shared this special status along with them and together they were termed as *azad qabayil*, that is, 'the free tribe'. This situation however; began to change in the last few decades when other groups gained military and political power in the civil war and started to impose claims on ethnic basis.

Overview of *Pashtunwali*

Pashtunwali is the most comprehensive and elaborate of the customary law systems in Afghanistan. *Pashtunwali* serves as a manual for the Pashtun population's way of life, social order, rights and obligations, morals and code of honour. The three primary pillars of *Pashtunwali* are *Enteqam, Pur* or *Badal* (right to revenge), *Melmasteya* (Hospitality) and *Nanawatia* (forgiveness). Pashtun honour is maintained by constant feuding revolving around *zar* (gold), *zan* (women) *and zameen* (land).[14] All these are based on the concept of *nang* or honour. According to Johnson and Mason, *nang* is not exactly analogous to the western concept of honour it can be described as 'representing a man's obligation to protect the inviolability of his person, his property and his women'.[15] *Nang* therefore means to defend one's rights and rights of one's tribe honourably. The Pashtun author Abdullah Bakhtani takes this idea to the point that 'a person who speaks Pashto but has no Pashtunwali is not a Pashtun, because other people also have learnt Pashto and speak it. Only a person who 'does Pashto' and follows its rules has *Pashtunwali*.[16] It would be interesting to engage with the three main concepts before proceeding further on *Pashtunwali*.

Enteqam, *Pur*, or Badal *(revenge)*

Badal is necessary in the event of an insult or injury to oneself or one family. Pakhtuns will take their revenge no matter how long it takes. Shahmahmood Miakhel mentions about a Pashto proverb, *Ka cheeri Pakhtun, khapal badal sal kala pas ham wakhle no beya ham-e-bera karay da*, meaning, if a Pashtun took his revenge after 100 years, it means that he is still in a hurry.[17] *Badal* also can be used to exchange girls to be married between families. A son grandson, great grandson or a cousin can take revenge even after several generations.[18] Patience in enacting revenge is seen in a positive light and folk stories hail those who waited years or decades to enact their vengeance. Vengeance can be invoked not only by violent acts, but merely challenging or even perceiving to challenge, the good name of a person or a tribe.[19]

One related aspect of *badal* is the family replacement mechanism, which is where younger members of a family feel obligated to step in for older fighters if the older is killed.[20] A younger man might be working while an older relative is away fighting, but will take up arms when the older relative is killed. In this case, the younger member of the family will go to the same unit that his relative served in. The purpose of this replacement system is to retain cohesion of the group. This system is particularly present in tribally based insurgent groups.[21]

Melmasteya (Hospitality)
Melmasteya obliges a Pashtun to provide for guest even unto his personal distress. Afghan hospitality is special because they try to extend it to all guests or visitors who come to their homes or villages even if they do not know them. A guest is offered the most sumptuous meal that a Pashtun can provide, given the best bed, pillow and quilt and waited on by all of the members of the host's families. A Pashtun does not need to know a guest's personal details to honour him generously.[22] The host will sit and chat with the guest as long as the guest wishes to converse.[23]

The first thing Afghans seek to build is their guesthouse (*Hujra*), which is a symbol of pride among families of villages. Many villages have a separate hut , which is called *hujra* and serves as a resting place for guest and travellers. The most important aspect of hospitality is protection of the guest. In rural areas of Afghanistan if a guest stays overnight, he is asked about his destination the next morning. If something happens to the guest in between destinations the family with who he stayed overnight has to defend his right. If the host family gets to know who robbed, dishonoured or killed the guest, they are obliged to take revenge on behalf of the guest.[24] Protection of guest is as important as protection of *namus*.

Nanawateya (forgiveness)

Nanawateya in Pashto literally means 'entering the house of the offender'. This ritual is performed in cases of attacks on a person's physical integrity (both killing and injury), when one of the feuding parties is too weak to take revenge or when bloodshed should be avoided for other reasons. Though in most cases, Pashtuns can only forgive their enemy and pass revenge if dispute is solved through Jirga. If a Jirga decided to send a delegation to victim's family, it is most likely that they will accept it and pardon the crime.[25] *Nanawatia* can be offered to those who seek protection and to even enemies who present themselves to their foes and surrender themselves. When *nanawateya* ritual is performed the offender gives the so called blood-money (*khunbaha*) to the family of victim (See Appendix: 1). It is the compensation for the inflicted damage and it is paid to avoid further revenge. The unit is called one *khun* (literally 'blood') or *nek* in some regions.[26] After the *Nanawateya* ritual has been accepted by the victim's family and the blood money has been paid to them, the blood fed must be stopped.

Some scholars argue that these concepts of *melamasteya and nanawatia* have changed in recent decades. Traditionally, if a foreigner is the cause of war, *Pashtunwali* does not require continuing with the two mentioned practices, but allows for a Pashtun to force out a guest. Mariam Abou Zahab argues 'tribal entrepreneurs' would honour foreign, especially Arab militants under the guise of *melamasteya* and *nanawatia,* but in actuality would get money from their 'guests' and use this to gain power and influence. These three pillars are certainly not the only aspects of *Pashtunwali*. Additional values those are important the codes are 'equality, respect, loyalty, pride, bravery, purdah, pursuit of romantic encounter, worship of Allah and unselfish love for friend'.[27]

Pashtunwali and Evolving of the Tribal Spirit

"Among the Pashtuns the word Pashtunwali implicates everything what ranks among the roots and basics of their tribal spirit, historical greatness and national traditions...Pashto is the name of their national language, Pashtun is the name of the tribe, Pashtunkhwa is the name of the homeland; and from these words the meaningful word Pashtunwali was created."[28]

According to Akbar Ahmed, the traditional tribal system of the Pashtuns consists of three major characteristics—descent from one common male ancestor, segmentary composition, and acephalous leadership.[29] The common or apical, male ancestor often gives his name to the tribe—for example, the Yusufzai tribe is descended from Yousuf or Ahmedzai tribe from Ahmed. Sometimes Pashtuns who live in a tribal area but who do not exactly have a blood relation tend to become subsumed in the dominant tribe and consider it to be their own.[30] Descent is always traced through male line and tribal organisation is patrilineal. Segmentary lineage means that society consists of parts; that branch out from a central 'trunk' and are related to one another. The individual is a member of a sub-section (*kor*), then section (*khel*), then a sub-clan (*beg*) and then a clan, a tribe and finally the entire Pashtun ethnic group, which is supposedly descended from Qais Abdur Rashid, who is said to have been the first Pashtun to have accepted Islam. Acephalous literally means 'without a head'; therefore, who has personal charisma and has the ability to give leadership, patronage on a battlefield or in times of stress gets to be the leader. This nature of tribal system leads some to discount the effectiveness of engaging with tribes in Afghanistan.[31]

The tribal system received severe shock in the 1970s with the beginning of Communist government, followed by the Soviet invasion and occupation, civil war, withdrawal of red army and rise and fall of Taliban. The Soviet occupation killed more than a million Pashtuns and created an additional three million refugees.[32] Displacement of so many Pashtuns into Pakistani refugee camps affected the tribal structure. Traditionally, the tribal leadership consisted of the tribal *khan or malik*, a representative of the government and *mullah* was the tribal religious leader. Position of *Khan* was substantially faded as no government official was present at refugee camps, leaving the *Mullahs* as the remaining authority figures. These refugee camps were often run by Deobandi and Salafi organisations that frequently channeled their aid through the mullahs. Thus, they became increasingly powerful and performed the function of leader that is providing patronage.[33]

Pakistan played a significant role in altering the tribal system as well. During Soviet intervention in Afghanistan; Pakistan could successfully position itself as a regional bulwark against communism and supplied the mujahedeen groups with the US funds and weaponry in order to tie down Communist Soviet Union. It is alleged that Pakistan used the struggle against Soviets and subsequent rise of Taliban to further its strategic goals in Afghanistan. Apart from repatriation of the refugees, and a desire for a friendly dispensation in Kabul that would provide Pakistan with 'strategic depth' vis-a vis India, another issue for meddling in Afghan affairs was the Pashtun factor. The Durrand Line which separated British Indian from Afghanistan divides Pashtuns between Pakistan and Afghanistan. Islamabad was concerned that Afghanistan coveted the Pashtun parts of Pakistan in NWFP, FATA and in Baluchistan. Therefore Pakistanis steered their support to groups and organizations that would emphasize Islamist identity as opposed to Pashtun nationalism.[34] Islamabad was aware of the fact that an irredentist Afghanistan and/or a strong movement from Khyber Pakhtunkhwa could very well threaten territorial integrity of Pakistan.

Traditionally a Mullah was the person who would call for *jihad* against foreign foes and unite tribes under the cause of defending religion but otherwise didn't have much political authority. They depended on the *maliks* for income and security. While these religious leaders used traditional tribal mechanism for securing power and patronage, they introduced change in the system. These leaders, who were generally products of Pakistani *madrasa*s, appealed to the concept of *Umma* or community of Islamic believers, and of ruling according to Islamic law or *Shari'ah*. They also pushed for the institution of *Shura* or a council made up of religious leaders as opposed to traditional *jirga*.[35] One of the distinctions between *jirga* and *shoura* is that, the former is more egalitarian and inclusive, and its decisions are normally advisory in nature while the *shoura's* decisions are directive and binding.[36]

Another effect of *madrasas* and refugee camps was that they brought Pashtuns from different tribes together and socialised them with non-tribal and religious environment.[37] The *'ulema* now became more effective force for communicating with and building networks between various tribes. These Pashtuns who received education from semi literate *mullahs* and grew up in camps didn't have much contact with their past and tradition. In the words of Ahmed Rashid:

> "These boys were a world apart from the Mujaheddin whom I had got to know during 1980s—me who could recount their tribal and clan lineages, remembered their abandoned farms and valleys with nostalgia and recounted legends and stories from Afghan history. These boys were from a generation who had never seen their country at peace—an Afghanistan not at war with invaders and itself. They had no memories of their tribes, their elders, their neighbours nor the complex ethnic mix of people that often made up their village and their homeland."[38]

While *madrasas* did contribute to a change in the tribal structure, the semi educated mullahs who often ran them taught a version of Islamic law or *Shari'ah* which was heavily influenced by Pashtunwali.[39]

Result was a group of warriors, much as they might have claimed to fight solely for Islam, still carried with them many of the social attitudes, beliefs and customs of Pashtuns. Thomas Rutting on the other hand believes, "every Pashtun knows which tribe, sub-tribe, 'clan' he or she belongs to. That cannot be destroyed even by social uprooting, displacement and urbanization."[40] He went on to explain how structure and behaviour of the Taliban especially recruitment, operations and succession is deeply rooted in Pashtun tribalism.[41]

Afghan Insurgency and *Pashtunwali*

The insurgency that was ushered in Afghanistan after 'Operation Enduring Freedom' was not a handiwork of Taliban alone, though there has been an increasing tendency to generalize every insurgency as Taliban activity. Groups under ex-mujahedeen commanders like Gulbuddin Hekmatyar, Jalaluddin Haqqani, Pakistan based groups like Lashkar-e-Toiba, Jamat-ud-Dawa, Jaish-e-Mohammad, and many others contributed significantly to it. Most of the insurgent networks cooperate with one another to a greater or lesser degree, therefore, determining the exact size of insurgency is not possible. Afghanistan experts have made educated guesses based on their research but those are at best an approximation of the real total. Eminent experts like Giustozzi and Kilcullen distinguish between core and non-core fighters. The later are recruited locally and operate on an ad hoc basis.[42] Kilcullen puts the number of potential reconcilable members at 90 per cent.[43] There is also a group of mercenaries forming an outer ring who undertake operations purely for monetary gain. These non-core fighters are the ones who are most susceptible to reconciliation and reintegration efforts.

The values of *Pashtunwali* influence the Afghan insurgency.[44] One of the contentions is that the Taliban could not surrender Osama bin Laden, as he was a guest under the Taliban's protection and to do so would have violated that pillar of *Pashtunwali* called

Nanawateya. Giving bin Laden up to the Americans would have resulted in the Taliban losing respect amongst its followers and thus negatively impact the Taliban's cohesion.[45] *Badal* fuels the insurgency by necessitating blood for Pashtuns who have been killed, whether they are innocent civilians or front line fighters. Johnson and Mason believes that the US cannot kill its way out of the insurgency, pointing to the fact that Soviets killed almost a million Pashtuns yet the numbers of guerrillas was greater at the end of the war than at the beginning.[46] In a research project conducted in Kandahar among Taliban members, almost third of the respondents had a family member killed by ISAF bombing and half of those respondents said they joined the insurgency after their family members were killed.[47]

ced*Pashtunwali*, Tribal Actors and Reconciliation Efforts
For Pashtuns collective justice that comes out of *jirga*, or assembly of tribe's adult male members is generally satisfactory. The *jirga* is a way for them to stop the cycle of *badal* and gives participants a way out with honour. Many tribal elders spoken to across the Southeast region stated that they could play a far more instrumental role than the government in bringing insurgents to the negotiation table, as they have long regarded themselves as being effective mediators.[48] In their opinion, only through traditional means of negotiations would peace be found, that is, through consultations and *jirgas* with impartial tribal elders and respected *'ulema* figures. The fact that this process was primarily overlooked by the international community, during the initial phase of intervention, is the reason behind the unsatisfying response according to some elderly Kabulis today.[49]

The other way of encouraging Taliban members to defect is the simple and longstanding one of bribing them. However this cannot be effective for the core group. Religious arguments could be used to reconcile and reintegrate insurgents and *Pashtunwali* can play a major role since it has a support base among tribal population. The initiation of the 'Qatar Process' by opening an office at Qatar for Taliban to negotiate with the US in January 2012 might as well have own ramifications.[50] Some of the Afghans view that this so called peace negotiation is not likely to go down well with their rural support base.[51] It was believed that with this step; negotiating some sort of power sharing deal with the Taliban is becoming a probable option even through no remarkable breakthrough between Karzai and Mullah Omar was an expected scenario. Overall perception suggested that even if Taliban were included at some level in the national or local government, they could be persuaded to lay down their arms. There are such precedents in Afghan history—for example, warlords such as General Dostum were given governorships of province and/or cabinet posts in exchange for their support of Afghan Government. However, the coordinated attacks on Kabul and three other provinces in mid-April 2012 by the Taliban indicated the resurgence of a stronger Taliban who might not be in a mood for any sort of compromise. Their stance was made amply clear when they called off the much talked about 'Qatar Process' in the response of Qur'an burning incident in Afghanistan in early 2012. The recent attacks also testified how the Afghan Security Forces played a vital role in countering the Taliban insurgents, along with Western Troops. While the country was regaining confidence on its security strength, President Karzai on the contrary was seen soft and non-critical of Taliban. There is a strong belief in Kabul that through such gestures the president wanted to ensure that the reintegration and reconciliation process that was commenced earlier does not come to a halt.

Conclusion
The tribal system of the Pashtuns has been beaten and battered over the past 30 years. The trauma of Soviet invasion, the refugee problem that was unleashed as a result of that, the Pakistani madrasas, the

influence of ISI and other agencies of Pakistani Government and the proxy war played by various other regional players; enhancing power and position of non-Pashtun tribes; weakened and changed the traditional tribal structure that was described by Ahmed Rashid and Lindholm.

At the end it must be remembered that *'Pashtunwali'* described an ideal, namely the ideal of the Pashtun way of life and ideals which seldom measure up to reality. Actual behaviour can be guided by several other values and factors.[52] In the past few decades, the Afghan society has experienced key changes. The society of Pashtun tribes is no longer the society that existed when most of the native accounts drawn on for writing research papers (by Western scholars) were written. War time situation after Soviet withdrawal and the military power of the commanders undermined the traditional hierarchy of Pashtun society as well as concept of equality.

This is not to suggest that tribal system has ceased to exist or has no relevance in contemporary Afghanistan. In some areas the tribes are stronger than other. Tribal system is particularly strong in areas were the central authority is relatively weaker. Even those Pashtuns who were raised in a detribalized environment in the refugee camps in Pakistan and who were taught by mullahs, still were inculcated with the traditional social norms and expectations of their culture. Those norms were based on *Pashtunwali*; it is just that they were packaged in an Islamic wrapper. While US-Taliban 'trust-building' process can be interpreted as a top-down mechanism to bring the situation in Afghanistan under control, the role of reconciliation and reintegration efforts under the banner of Afghan government, involving the traditional tribal actors is supposed to provide a parallel, bottom-up and perhaps more effective mechanism that may complement the other process. Whatever might be the outcome, the Afghan government quite evidently is not in a position to scrap its 'reconciliation and reintegration' tool at this moment. Therefore the question about the importance of *Pashtunwali* in modern Afghanistan cannot be answered in any general way. Today it faces competition from other value systems which have gained importance in the last few decades. Indeed, the values guiding the behaviour of individuals or groups are largely dependent of a particular situation. Yet it might not be wrong to say, among current competing value systems, the ideal of *Pashtunwali* still present an attractive option today.

Appendix: 1

Figure 1: The Blood Money of Ahmedzai tribe (source: Khadim, Pashtunwali, pp-183)		
Killing		
Premeditated murder		2 Khun
Manslaughter		1 Khun
Injuries Spin – 'white (visible) body parts'		
Eye	1 eye, Both eye	½ Khun, 1 Khun
Nose		½ Khun
Tongue		1 Khun
Teeth	Every visible tooth/ Nonvisible tooth	1/10 the of a Khun/Special Blood Money
Legs	One leg/both legs	½ Khun/1 Khun
Arms and Hand	One arm/hand, both arms /hands	½ khun, 1 Khun (Blood money can differ is case when only the part below the elbow is lost)
Fingers	Thumb or all four bearing fingers on one hand	1 khun
	Thumbs or all for bearing fingers on both hands	2 Khuns

Notes

1. Favre Raphy, "Interface between State and Society in Afghanistan, discussion on key social features affecting governance, reconciliation and reconstruction." February 2005. http://www.aizon.org/Administration%20and%20society%20in%20Afghanistan.pdf
2. Vern Leibl, "Pushtuns, Tribalism, Leadership, Islam and Taliban: A short View". *Small Wars and Insurgencies.* vol. 18, no. 3, September 2007, p. 492.
3. Lutz Rzehak, "Doing Pashto", *Afghanistan Analysts Network*. 2001. http://www.humansecuritygateway.com/documents/AAN_DoingPashto.pdf
4. Ahmed Rashid, *Descent Into Chaos : How war against Extremism is being lost in Pakistan, Afghanistan and Central Asia*, (London, Penguin Books, 2008).
5. Rzehak, "Doing Pashto".
6. Ibid.
7. Ibid, p. 16.
8. Ibid.
9. Shahahmood Miakhel, "The Importance of Tribal structures and *Pakhtunwali* in Afghanistan: Their role is security and governance" in Arpita Basu Roy, (ed) *Challenges and Dilemmas of State-Building in Afghanistan,* (New Delhi: Shipra Publication, 2008).
10. Montstuart Elphinstone, "An Account of the Kingdom of Caubul," (Karachi: Indus Publication (2 volumes), 1992), p. 220.
11. Rzehak, op. cit.
12. Wesh Zalmiyan (Awakened Youths') appeared as a rather informal movement in 1947 under the leadership of Mohammad Rasul khan Pashtun. From 1951 publications on the political agenda of this movement appeared in the newspaper Angar. The main ideal of the movement was patriotism. Education, national unity and participation of people in political affairs were seen as main ways to lead people of Afghanistan out of 'darkness of ignorance'.
13. Lutz, Ibid, p. 6.
14. Rashid, *Descent Into Chaos*.
15. Johnson and Mason, "No Sign Until the Burst of Fire: Understanding the Pakistan-Afghanistan Frontier", *International Security*, vol. 32, no. 4, 2008.
16. Rzehak, op. cit., p. 9.
17. Miakhel, op. cit.
18. Ibid.
19. Major Jim Gant, "One Tribe at a Time: A strategy for Success in Afghanistan", (Los Angeles, CA, Nine Sisters Imports, 2009).
20. Smith Graeme, "What Kandahar's Taliban Say?" in Antonio Giustozzi(ed),, *Decoding the New Taliban: Insights from the field*, (New York: Columbia

University Press, 2009).
21. Amato Jonathan, "Tribes, Pashtunwali and How they impact Reconciliation and Reintegration Efforts in Afghanistan", (Washington, DC: Georgetown University Press, 2010).
22. Rzehak, Ibid, p-15.
23. Jonathan. Ibid.
24. Miakhel, Ibid.
25. Ibid.
26. Rzehak, op. cit., pp.15-19.
27. Jonathan. op. cit., p. 21.
28. Rzehak, op. cit., p. 7.
29. Akbar S. Ahmed, *Social and Economic Change in the Tribal Areas 1972-1976*, (Oxford: Oxford University Press, 1977), pp. 14-17.
30. Ibid, p. 14.
31. Jonathan, op. cit.
32. Johnson and Mason, "No Sign Until the Burst of Fire".
33. Jonathan, Ibid.
34. Ahmed Rashid, *Taliban: Militant Islam, Oil and Fundamentalism in Central Asia,* (New Haven: Yale University Press, 2000).
35. Roy Oliver, "Afghanistan: Back to Tribalism or on to Lebanon?" *Third World Quarterly,* vol. 11, no. 4, October 1989.
36. Jonathan, Ibid.
37. Graeme Smith, "What Kandahar's Taliban Say?" in Decoding the New Taliban: Insights from the field, Antonio Giustozzi. (ed), (New York: Columbia University Press, 2009).
38. n. 34.
39. Ibid.
40. Rutting Thomas, "The Other Side: Dimensions of the Afghan Insurgency: Causes, Actors and Approaches to "Talks" *Afghanistan Analysts Network.* Thematic Report, 2009.
41. Ibid
42. Antonio Giustozzi, *Koran, Kalashnikov and Laptop: The Neo-Taliban Insurgency in Afghanistan*, (New York: Columbia University Press, 2009). pp-33-34.
43. David Kilcullen, *The Accidental Guerrilla: Fighting Small Wars in the Midst of a Big One*. (Oxford: Oxford University Press, 2009).
44. Jonathan, Ibid.
45. Ibid.
46. Thomas H. Johnson and M. Chris Mason, "Understanding the Taliban and the Insurgency in Afghanistan". *Orbis,* vol. 51, no. 1, 2007.
47. Smith, op. cit, 2009.

48. "Reconciliation and Reintegration in Loya Paktia", *TLO Policy Brief*, October 2010.
49. Interview with some of the elderly Kabulis were conducted in Karte Parwan (Kabul) by the author during her field trip to Afghanistan, April 02, 2012.
50. " Taliban in 'trust-building process with US in Qatar". *The National*, January 30, 2012. http://www.thenational.ae/news/world/middle-east/taliban-in-trust-building-process-with-us-in-qatar
51. Openion was shared by few Afghans on condition of anonymity. Interview was conducted by the author between April 01-05, Kabul, Afghanistan.
52. Rzehak, op. cit, p.20.

8. Economic Impact of Terrorism: Case of South Asia Post 9/11

Anindya Sengupta and Anshuman Tiwari

A year after 9/11, the Comptroller of the City of New York gave a report[1] on the economic consequences of the most audacious terror attack ever. The report pegged the property losses at US$ 21.4 billion, and the attack on twin towers itself was described as a direct attack on the heart of American capitalism. Although the figure appears a large one, it was but a minor red mark seen in the context of the US national economy, at just 0.2 per cent of annual GDP. Around 2800 people died in the terrible tragedy—in a rather chilling accounting of the cost of a human (rather American) life, the report calculates the total cost of lives lost at US$ 8.7 billion and cost due to disability at US$ 0.9 billion.[2] But then, in the most significant part of the report, it observes that there was a large economic loss for the city in terms of diversion of business, which is difficult to quantify. It clearly makes the point why we need to study the economic consequences of terrorism in detail—simply because what is reported in next day's newspaper is just the direct cost of an attack. Direct cost of a terror attack—in terms of lives lost or damage to property at the site—is undoubtedly the most spectacular part of it but often proves to be the tip of the iceberg in terms of its economic consequences. Due to increased terror activity in any region, investment goes down and in the long run income and consumption also go down; thus terror, specially repeated terror activities, have significant economic fallout.

Terrorism by definition is asymmetric warfare. An act of terror is different from an ordinary criminal or violent act only because of the intent behind it. An individual terrorist or a group tries to inflict maximum physical damage directly during an attack but the strategy of any terrorist group is to bleed its perceived opponent (state or society) through thousand cuts—therefore, they try to maximize the long term or indirect cost through such attacks.

It was only after 9/11, the study of economic consequences of terrorism attracted scholarly attention in the West. Through recent research, three distinct components in terms of economic consequences of a terror attack have been identified—direct, indirect and frictional.[3] It is however important to remember the context of such analysis—apart from three cases, the Basque region of Spain, Northern Ireland and Israel—Western world has so far witnessed only isolated cases of violence. Violence due to long term militancy with sustained attack on socio-economic infrastructure obviously produces a different set of pattern. South Asia is the only region in the world to have witnessed this kind of terrorism in the last two decades. In South Asia, the very context of post-9/11 world provides a definite break with the past terror-induced violence.

Though South Asia is one of the worst affected regions in terms of terrorist violence but to the best of our knowledge there has not been any comprehensive study on the subject. Purpose of the current paper is to present a preliminary analysis of the South Asian scenario, and also to examine to what extent this scenario could be analyseanalysed through the methodology established in the West. Though the economic impact of other types of violence like insurgency in some of the North-Eastern states and ultra-left wing violence in some other Indian states may be fundamentally similar in nature, it is due to the specific context of post 9/11 world that we have restricted the scope of this present study to a much smaller geographical area.[4] Similarly, a comprehensive study of economic impact of terrorism in South Asia must also include left-wing violence in Nepal and ethnic violence in Sri Lanka.[5] Also, the aim of this paper is only to study the economic consequences of terrorism and not the whole economy that sustains such terrorism/terror infrastructure.

The Western Template
Basic economic impact of a single act of terrorism or a series of terror attacks is similar to that of a criminal act. First, there is a direct cost in terms of lives lost and property damaged just like in case of arson or murder. Next, a series of attacks at a particular neighbourhood or increased possibility of such attacks puts pressure on law enforcement mechanism—they are forced to deploy more resources to secure the place. This is indirect cost, which very often is much higher than the actual material damage. Second, comes a somewhat intractable category of cost—in terms of distorted decisions—even if a district had all the right potential still high rate of crime is more likely to depress property prices there. Productive people are likely to move out of the district and new investors would shy away from the crime-infested area—it is difficult to put an estimate for such lost opportunities and also once the image is maligned in such a way, it takes a long while before attracting back the right crowd or investment there.

Direct Cost is the easiest part of the calculations. This is fundamentally similar to accidents or natural calamities. The key components for calculating the direct cost of a terror attack are number of human lives lost, extent of damage to property at the site of the attack and the cost of rescue, relief and immediate dislocation. Businesses like airlines, travel and tourism also bear the direct brunt of such attacks. A Congressional Report citing the US Bureau of Labour Statistics mentioned that at least 1,25,000 workers across the US were laid off for 30 or more days because of 9/11.[6] A Milken Institute Study estimated potential job loss in 2002 in the metropolitan US due to 9/11 to be around 1.6

million.[7] 9/11 also hit the headlines as the largest insured losses in history till then with an estimated loss between US$ 36 and US$ 54 billion.[8]

Indirect cost due to terrorist attacks has also been described as terror tax.[9] To prevent recurrence of such attacks, a state or society invests heavily in deterrent mechanisms. As the resources are limited, therefore the concerned state or society is compelled to divert necessary resources from other areas, more often from developmental expenditure or social sector like health and education. But first it is difficult to calculate the precise amount of loss and then it is even more difficult to draw the line. If we look at the post 9/11 scenario of businesses moving out of downtown New York, it could also be because of high property prices or broken infrastructure or high taxation or a combination of several such factors. 9/11 attacks or a sense of insecurity might have played a part in it but it is difficult to emphatically say that businesses moved out solely due to the 9/11 attacks. Secondly, even if we assume businesses moved out post 9/11 then does it actually represent a net loss to the economy? As long as they are within the US, there is no such loss for the national economy (though it would still be a loss for the New York City economy), some might even argue that such movements away from New York would lead to more geographically balanced economic development.

9/11 definitely led to a huge increase in defence and internal security spending. Afghan war was a direct consequence of that. War in Iraq cannot be technically called a direct consequence but surely without 9/11 it would have been immensely difficult to justify invasion of Iraq. However, the fact that even after 10 years, the US exchequer is still allocating so much resource for Afghanistan and Iraq—can it be counted solely as an indirect cost of 9/11? Narrow security-centric worldview in last 10 years has led to dilution of US economic hegemony, but definitely, it would be too far-fetched to count this solely as an indirect cost of 9/11.

But what exactly has been the quantum of increase in terms of defence and homeland security spending? Between 2001 and 2011, the US spent a mind-numbing US$ 7.2 trillion for defence and homeland security—this includes the cost of Iraq and Afghan wars and that section of the budget of Department of Energy, which is related to Nuclear weapons. Pentagon base budget itself (i.e. excluding the cost of two wars) has gone up by 43 per cent since 2001. Department of Homeland Security, which was created in the wake of 9/11 attacks, started off with a budget of US$ 16 billion, in next ten years it has gone up by more than 300 per cent.

Table 1

	2001 (US$)	2011 (US$)	Increase (%)
Pentagon Base budget	290.5 bn	526.1 bn	43
Homeland security	16 bn	69.1 bn	301
Total	7.2 trillion (2001-11)		

Source: Congressional Budget Office, CBO

As per the report of the City Comptroller, the direct and calculable cost of 9/11 was around US$ 30 billion but as the above table shows the real cost to American economy was many times more. Remember this was after all just one attack, in case of sustained terrorist attacks over a period of time any economy significantly loses momentum. In case of Israel, it is clearly shown through analysis of quarterly data that how due to terror, government expenditure on security increased and correspondingly private consumption declined (Eckstein & Tsiddon, 2004).[10] Analysing a 3-year period (2000-03) during the Al Akza Intifada, the authors conclude that there is a fall of 3 per cent annually in per capita output. During this period, per capita GDP and non-durable consumption also show a fall of around 3.5 per cent each. Defence Expenditure on the other hand jumps from 9 per cent of GDP to 12 per cent during the same period.¹¹ Similarly, in case of Spain, it has been shown that the Basque region is about 10 per cent poorer than it would be in the absence of the terrorist group ETA.¹²

Friction Economy: In a widely read cover story in 2002, business magazine *Fortune* concluded that the real cost of 9/11 should be measured in terms of response to terrorism, and how it has generated frictions all over the great American economic machine.¹³ *Fortune* estimated a loss of 1.5 per cent of GDP per annum due to these frictional costs. First of these friction costs was in form of massive hikes in insurance premium—in fact, there was no template of terror insurance in most of the western economies and the current matrix of premium calculations came in vogue only as a consequence of 9/11. Since 9/11 significantly pushed up the cost of this type of insurance, many important structures—like Golden Gate Park, San Francisco—were unable to get terror insurance. This led the US Congress to pass the Terrorism Risk Insurance Act, TRIA to address any possible market failure due to such large scale risk. Under this act, the US government is mandated to pay the insurers up to 85 per cent of their losses. It has now been extended up to 2014 as Terrorism Risk Insurance Program Authorization Act, TRIPA.¹⁴

The second and the biggest chunk of increase as described by the magazine is a contestable one. *Fortune* claimed that the attacks have compelled businesses to review their supply chain management system and in place of just-in-time delivery they have been forced to stock up supplies to mitigate any unforeseen situation. The magazine argued that this raw material holding cost in turn had significantly slowed down the US productivity. Most subsequent studies have rejected this contention though they have agreed on enhanced transaction cost due to heightened security. The magazine also showed that for a passenger, average waiting time at the US airports went up by one hour, which straightaway shaves off 0.1 per cent of US GDP per annum! No doubt, extra security measures and distorted decision-making were responsible for significant loss of productivity in aggregate terms but the magazine seems to have overstated the case.

Terror in South Asia

South Asia is not only one of the worst affected regions in terms of terrorism; statistics also shows that terrorism related incidents have gone up here sharply since mid-1990s. Four countries in this region—India, Pakistan, Sri Lanka, and Nepal are among the worst affected countries in the world during this period.

Global Terrorism Database, being maintained by the University of Maryland,[15] shows that during 1970s and 1980s, the major victims were Central and Latin American states. But from mid-1990s South Asia along with Middle East occupy the two top slots. The chart also shows a sharp rise from 2007-08 due to increased militant attacks in North-West Pakistan and clashes of Sri Lankan army with the LTTE, eventually leading to a military defeat of LTTE. The two most important takeaways from all these statistics are (1) terrorism in South Asia is a long-term issue and the region as a whole, and (2) India and Pakistan in particular have been facing unending series of attacks, resulting in significant loss of lives and damage to physical and socio-economic infrastructure.

Table 2: Global Terrorism 1970-2007

Most Frequently Attacked		Most Fatalities	
Country	Frequency	Country	Fatality Count
Colombia	6767	Iraq	17754
Peru	6038	Sri Lanka	14272
El Salvador	5330	India	13434
India	4318	Colombia	13009
Northern Ireland	3762	Peru	12822
Spain	3165	El Salvador	12496
Iraq	3161	Nicaragua	11324
Turkey	2691	Algeria	8545
Sri Lanka	2611	Philippines	6304
Pakistan	2536	Pakistan	5540
Philippines	2490	Guatemala	5135
Chile	2287	Turkey	4674
Israel	2140	Burundi	4084
Guatemala	2023	Afghanistan	3764
Nicaragua	1986	United States	3339
South Africa	1921	Rwanda	3200
Lebanon	1913	Lebanon	3093
Algeria	1650	Russia	3057
Italy	1487	Angola	2861
United States	1362	Northern Ireland	2842

Source: Global Terrorism Database

Chart 1 – GTD data rivers: Global Terrorism Database

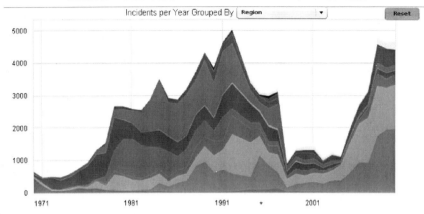

Name	Count
Middle East & North Africa	18638
South America	17563
South Asia	17357
Western Europe	14784
Central America & Caribbean	10548
Sub-Saharan Africa	6400
Southeast Asia	6004
North America	2849
Russia & the Newly Independent States (NIS)	1925
Central America & Caribbean	10548
Sub-Saharan Africa	6400
Southeast Asia	6004
North America	2849
Russia & the Newly Independent States (NIS)	1925
Eastern Europe	906
East Asia	687
Australasia & Oceania	232
Central Asia	219

Direct Cost of Terror in South Asia

As we have already mentioned direct cost implies lives lost in attacks, damage to property and damage to business due to such attacks. Apart from businesses, which are generally affected all over the world immediately after a terrorist attack—airlines, hotels and tourism—in South Asia, there has been a particular emphasis on transportation sector. Trains and railway networks in particular have been the repeated targets of terrorists across the subcontinent.[16]

It is important to analyse how these material losses actually impact the economy as a whole. There are two important parameters for doing so – we need to see the loss of human lives in terms of loss per million populations and the cost due to other material losses need to be measured in proportion to the country's GDP. These two indices help us to understand proportionate impact on the economy and society. Just to illustrate the point, a loss of US$ 30 billion may not make much difference to the US economy but it would inflict crippling blows to a small economy like Nepal.

Global terrorism database records that between 1968 and 2004, there were a total of 16,730 terror-related incidents. 10.9 per cent of these incidents took place in Israel, making it the most vulnerable country in terms of terror attacks. India with a share of 6.6 per cent is the second most vulnerable country. Out of a total recorded 94,628 fatalities and injuries, again Israel tops the list with 10.6 per cent share. India is at the third place with a share of 8.2 per cent of fatalities and injuries. But to actually understand the impact of these tragic statistics, one needs to look at the respective size of India's and Israel's population—for every million of its population, Israel recorded 258 terrorist attacks as against just one incident per million people in India. Israel suffered 1,502 casualties per million people; in the case of India it was just 7. In terms of economic impact, it is more important to look at incidents per billion dollars of GDP statistics—here tiny Lebanon tops the chart and in case of India—despite far higher casualties, hardly makes an impact. Exactly for the same reasons, the present cycle of violence as witnessed from 2006-07 onwards is proving to be far more debilitating for Pakistan.

Table 3: Terror Statistics (1968-2004)

	Total No of terrorist incidents (1968-2004)/% of total 16,730 incidents	Total fatalities & injuries/% of total 94,628	No of terrorist incidents/ million population	Fatalities & injuries/ million population	No of terrorist incidents / **GDP 1 billion US$**
Top Country	Israel (10.9)	Israel (10.6)	Israel (258)	Israel (1,502)	Lebanon (35)
India	6.6 (Rank 2)	8.2 (Rank 3)	1	7	2
Pakistan	2.85 6.5 (Rank 5) 3			42	6

Source: Global Terrorism Database

The next chart, which tracks the same statistics for next 6 years (2005-11) clearly brings out the gravity of the situation in Pakistan.

Chart 2: South Asia (2005-11)

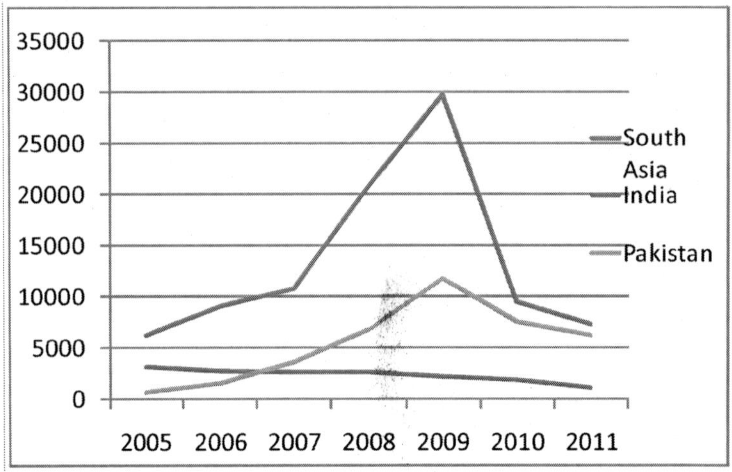

[Line chart showing South Asia, India, and Pakistan data from 2005 to 2011, with y-axis from 0 to 35000. South Asia peaks around 30000 in 2009.]

Source: Global Terrorism Database

The sharp rise in 2008-09 is due to high casualty figures in anti-LTTE operations in Sri Lanka. But other than that terrorism-related incidents have gone up very sharply in Pakistan during this period. On the other hand, India has been witnessing a steady decline—in fact, there have been considerably less violence in recent years in some of the long-standing trouble-spots like the North-East and Kashmir valley (though incidents outside these areas have gone up).

Though one can get a reasonably accurate picture in terms of human costs, it is difficult to arrive at a correct estimate of property losses. One of the main reasons for that is lack of insurance penetration in a poor region like South Asia. But it is possible to present some analysis of the actual economic impact of terrorism in South Asia. To have a closer look, we propose to look at three different levels—macro-level (that of a province or region), city level and at micro level like a particular industry segment. In our understanding, terrorism so far has not become a large enough problem for the Indian economy as a whole. On the other hand, the recent wave of terror in Pakistan has seriously dented the country's economy and this admission comes from the Pakistan government itself. In 2010-11, Pakistan Economic Survey carried a special chapter on how the war on terror is bleeding the economy white.[17] The cost for anti-militancy operations went up from US$ 2.72 billion (2001-02) to US$ 17.82 billion (2010-11). Thus, a poor country like Pakistan was forced to spend a total of US$ 68 billion between 2001 and 2011. Travel ban by most of the western countries along with general insecurity led to a precipitous fall in investment and trade. Terror and trade is always inversely correlated—textile export almost slumped in Pakistan as foreign buyers refused to travel to the country or open letter of credit facilities with Pakistani banks. Widespread violence directly led to a sharp rise in insurance premium, effectively shutting foreign capital and industry out of Pakistan.[18] In the North-West frontier (Khyber Pakhtunkhwa) and FATA, millions were displaced, physical infrastructure was destroyed and travel and tourism came to a virtual halt leading to massive job losses. In 2009, after the global credit crisis, Pakistan's growth rate plummeted to just 2 per cent and as most observers have noticed threat of terrorism and anti-terror operations were equally or perhaps more responsible for the crisis than global turmoil. The result was best summarized in the Economic Survey itself: "Pakistan has never witnessed such devastating social & economic upheaval in its industry, even after dismemberment of the country by direct war."[19]

Impact at Provincial Level

One of the most distinguishing features of terrorism in South Asia is its duration—in a number of places, a large area is held hostage to terrorism for a considerable period. Kashmir Valley in India and in recent times NWFP-FATA in Pakistan are examples of how local economy is either destroyed or severely distorted due to long and intensive terrorism. The unique reality of Kashmir is that now for more than two decades it has been witnessing terrorist violence at a level, which is much more intensive than isolated attacks but at a level lower than an open civil war. Between 1989 (when terrorism broke out in the valley) and 2011, Kashmir has witnessed as many as 17 years of high density violence, resulting in more than 1000 fatalities a year.[20] This high level of physical violence resulted in sharp increase in both direct (destruction of property, infrastructure and displacement of people) and indirect cost (policing cost, deployment of army and paramilitary, terror tax on business and individuals). This long phase of violence virtually destroyed Kashmir's tourism business. There were specific attacks on Bengali tourists (largest domestic group of tourists in the valley) and a number of foreign tourists were kidnapped. Kashmir's famed handicraft industries like hand-woven carpets, shawls, papier mache virtually collapsed. Growers of a number of fruits and cash crops like apples, saffron went out of business. Roads fell into disrepair and power supply all but broke down due to targeted attacks and difficulty in maintenance. The following two tables may be helpful in understanding the effect of such physical violence in the valley, home to an estimated 5.5 million people:

Table 3: Loss of Lives in Kashmir

Year	Incidents	Security Forces Killed	Civilians Killed	Terrorists Killed
2003	3,401	314	795	1,494
2004	2,565	281	707	976
2005	1,990	189	557	917
2006	1,667	151	389	591
2007	1,092	110	158	472
2008	708	75	91	339
2009	499	79	71	239
2010	488	69	47	232
2011	340	33	31	100

Source: Home Ministry *Annual Report* of different years. Before 2003, figures are mentioned according to financial year, that is, 2002-03, therefore, difficult to compare with later figures. SATP gives a complete table from 1988 to till date but figures are quite different

Table 4: Destruction of Property by Militants in Jammu & Kashmir

Year	Total Incidents	Govt. Buildings	Educational Buildings	Private House	Bridges	Shops	Hospitals
1990	646	501	129	1,242	172	202	0
1991	391	45	24	819	24	83	0
1992	564	65	57	2,312	28	200	0
1993	662	98	46	1,110	34	400	0
1994	606	172	119	666	46	162	4
1995	688	127	133	1,814	16	402	2
1996	482	52	68	602	2	161	3
1997	259	13	11	437	5	67	1
1998	177	13	15	273	1	66	0
1999	136	7	9	284	2	6	0
2000	129	14	6	330	1	107	0
2001	274	30	16	419	2	77	1
2002	255	14	10	421	4	20	0
Total	5268	1151	643	10,729	337	1,953	11

Source: Government of India, Ministry of Home Affairs, *Annual Report 2002-03*, p. 13.

Apart from outright destruction, a long period of violence actually introduces long term distortions in the economy. There was no dearth of fund flow into Kashmir during this period. During the decade of 1991-2000, Srinagar was one of the rare Indian cities to have witnessed sharp rise in property prices. A New York Times report in 2002 claimed that '......there are 21,000 cars in Srinagar alone—a fivefold increase from 1990. There were 560 private schools in the valley seven years ago; there are 1,360 now..... No one knows how much money for militants, carried in person or passed on through bank deposits, has come into the state. Some suspect that at least some of that money has been channeled through Jammu and Kashmir Bank, the most successful institution in the state and the most vivid emblem of Kashmir's boom. Since militancy began, its deposits have grown from US$ 458 million to US$ 2.29 billion'.[21] Central government poured in more funds than ever before,[22] there were aids from outside and then, there were clandestine supply from across the border through separatist elements. However, these funds could not be channelised through productive economic routes due to terrorism. Instead these funds helped to strengthen the distortion in the economy. Typically even after militancy ends, a state takes a long time to come back to economic mainstream—for example, Punjab or Assam—due to prevalence of these distortions in the economic structures.

Two regions of Pakistan—North West Frontier Province (now Khyber Pakhtunkhwa) and Federally Administered Tribal Areas or FATA—have witnessed unprecedented violence since 2005-06. Our purpose is not to trace the root of this violence but this is directly connected with the so-called war on terror. Through suicide bombings, use of fatal explosives, militants in these two areas have inflicted massive casualties on security forces and common men. Retaliation by the Army has sparked off more violence and resulted in more fatalities. Militants here have deliberately targeted business and economic infrastructure. In addition, they have also launched a ruthless attack on educational institutions—as a part of their strategy to implement their ideology through theological seminaries rather than secular schools—destroying or damaging as many as 65 per cent schools in Swat Valley alone. The economic cost of such attacks will have to be borne by future generations too. Swat, like Kashmir Valley, was a premier tourist destination. There were more than 800 hotels in Swat alone employing more than 40,000 people in the hospitality sector—most of these hotels went out of business and people lost their livelihood as tourism economy of Swat almost collapsed.[23] Similarly fruit economy of Malakand and Swat are on the verge of collapse. Violence has displaced more than 3 million people in these two areas—this has put a huge strain on the entire Pakistan economy. Even when the violence subsides, it will take many years to rebuild/repair these losses.[24]

What we have been discussing so far is the economic consequences of a terror attack from a victim's point of view. There is also a cost of harbouring terror—Benmelech, Berrebi and Klor in their paper on economic impact of suicide bombing have presented robust evidence for cost of harbouring terror.[25] According to their calculations, a single successful suicide attack in Israel results in 5.3 per cent increase in unemployment and significantly set back the home district of the concerned Palestinian suicide bomber at least for next six months. Pakistan, like India and other countries is definitely a victim of terror but it is also paying an additional cost of harbouring terror.

A Tale of Two Cities

Terrorism is essentially an urban phenomenon. City as we all know, apart from being a societal melting pot, which is often volatile, also is the growth engine of any economy. The connection therefore is quite obvious. Since the basic intention of any terrorist organisation is to inflict maximum damage, they are better off targeting congested urban areas where density of both population and productivity is maximum. Among all the major cities and capitals around the world, three South Asian cities have been hit most number of times by terrorists—Kabul, Karachi and Mumbai. Since this article is more about India and Pakistan, we will limit ourselves to Mumbai and Karachi. There are many similarities between these two cities— right from pre-independence days they have been described as sister cities—both are port cities with mixed population and with huge hinterlands. Since 1947, both have been commercial capitals of their respective nations.

Bombay or Mumbai is an intriguing city. From the early 1990s or more specifically since the Babri Masjid demolition in 1992, Mumbai and every sphere of Mumbai life from underworld to Bollywood has been under the shadow of terrorism. Various connections involving terror organisations and incidents are too well known to be repeated here but the table provided below captures the regularity of terror attacks in India's largest and the most important urban centre in last two decades:

Sl. No.	Date	Place	Killed	Injured
1	March 12, 1993	13 blasts across the city	257	713
2	August 28, 1997	Near Jama Masjid	0	3
3	January 24, 1998	Malad	0	1
4	February 27, 1998	Virar	9	0
5	December 02, 2002	Ghatkopar	3	31
6	December 06, 2002	Mumbai Central railway station	0	25
7	January 27, 2003	Vile Parle	1	25
8	March 13, 2003	Mulund Railway Station	11	80
9	April 14, 2003	Bandra	1	0
10	July 29, 2003	Ghatkopar	3	34
11	August 25, 2003	Gateway of India and Zaveri Bazaar	52	160
12	July 11, 2006	7 blasts at 7 locations in local trains across the city	181	890
13	November 26, 2008	Multiple terrorist attacks across the city	166	300
14	July 13, 2011	Serial blasts in Mumbai	26	131
Total			710	2,393

Source: South Asia Terrorism Portal, http://www.satp.org/

Every time there was a serial blast or isolated blasts in Mumbai, regular targets included suburban railway, which is the lifeline of Mumbai, stock market and diamond trading centres. On November 26, 2008, when the most daring terror attack took place, two of the city's most important hotels were the prime targets, in addition to the main railway station. Bombay Stock Market came to a standstill when it was attacked in 1993 but since then stock trading has largely moved on to computer screens and thus has become largely location-neutral—today a blast or serial blasts in Mumbai affects the stock market the way any other disaster does but does not bring trading to a halt. Similarly major stock traders or companies have also fanned out across the city rather than staying around congested Dalal Street. The story of diamond industry is somewhat different—just like the Bombay stock Exchange, Bombay diamond hub, which is centred around Zaveri Bazaar-Opera House (target of attack even in 2011) has been the target of repeated attacks. A large number of diamond traders, who are predominantly Gujarati Jains and Hindus—have already shifted base to Gujarat (Surat, Ahmedabad), which they consider a safer option. Some of the traders have also shifted or are in the process of shifting to Bharat Diamond Bourse in Bandra-Kurla, leaving the South Mumbai diamond hub bereft of its former glory.

It is, however, important to strike the right balance while measuring the actual impact of terrorist attacks on the economy of Mumbai. Some of the businesses are shifting out of Mumbai due to many reasons, including very high cost of real estate (highest in the country and one of the costliest office spaces anywhere in the world); general lack of security in a congested, unplanned city is one of the factors there but not always the only factor. Similarly newspaper headlines in praise of so-called Mumbai spirit or resilience of the city the day after a blast appear to be overdone. In most cases people come out or board the same train, which was the target previous day, not as a conscious protest against terrorism but simply because they do not have an option. Mumbai in economic terms is no longer the sole growth engine of a resurgent Indian economy. Mumbai city has largely missed the software bus. By contrast, Pune, apart from its manufacturing focus, appears to have claimed the pole position in terms of new economy in the region. Pune, traditionally the gentle-paced small town and Marathi cultural capital, has emerged in the last two decades as a knowledge economy hub. As Pune emerged as a destination for many an IT company and ambitious youngsters, terror followed on close heels—German bakery blast on February 13, 2010 killed 17 people and injured at least 60, including foreigners.

Similarly, Karachi is Pakistan's most populous city and it is more important to Pakistan's economy compared to what Mumbai is to Indian economy. Karachi city alone accounts for more than 50 per cent of Pakistan's total revenue collection and it contributes more than 20 per cent to the nation's GDP. Karachi port, the most important commercial channel for the Pakistani economy, accounts for more than 60 per cent of trade (Karachi and Port Qasim together handle more than 90 per cent of Pakistan's cargo traffic). In 2010, all four provincial capitals in Pakistan were among the worst affected cities in the country in terms of terror attacks. 44 people were killed in Lahore, 111 in Peshawar and 189 in Quetta. But the level of violence in Karachi was far more damaging than all these cities put together. In 2011, all the terror-related casualties in Sindh province were reported from Karachi city. As per SATP database, the total casualty in 2011 in Karachi was 1048.[26] As per the other available source, CRSS,[27] the figure stands at 1,675. There are many shades of violence in Karachi—political, ethnic and routine criminal or hooligan violence. These have often resulted in huge number of targeted killings apart from regular suicide bombings and bomb blasts. Entire Pakistan appears to be paying a very high economic cost for terrorism but Karachi city seems to be worst affected simply because more business has traditionally been concentrated here and it has more potential than other places.

Impact at Micro Level

We have already discussed about the impact of terrorism at the provincial and city level. Targeted terror has also impacted certain industries and places at the grass root level as well, inflicting severe economic hardship on people associated with the place/trade. Most evidences in this category are, however, essentially anecdotal in nature. Before terrorism peaked, Kashmir was known for its cricket bats made from local Willow tree. This thriving industry all but collapsed due to security problem. The industry eventually over the years has shifted base to Punjab. Manufacturers in Punjab use the same wood but value addition is now done outside Kashmir. We have already mentioned how diamond business is moving away from its traditional hub in South Mumbai. Similarly certain areas in a metropolitan city have seen property prices dipping or business straying away as there is a general sense of insecurity. This again as discussed in case of New York may not be a net negative for the economy but for local economy and local people often it proves to be a crippling blow. Similarly for businessmen and companies and communities at individual level cost of an attack or destruction is often borne even years after the actual damage is done. Rebuilding Taj hotel or Oberoi in Mumbai is costly but may not pose a serious challenge for their owners. But rebuilding a monument or even individual business involves huge cost often almost impossible for their owners to bear—this assumes special significance in the context of absence of insurance.

Indirect Cost in South Asia
Indirect cost of terrorism in South Asia needs to be seen in two separate categories—one is the tax to the government and the second is in terms of terror tax to individuals and businesses. Forced resource diversion—mainly from development sectors to security—is the biggest drain on exchequer. Compared to a developed country like the US, this forced resource diversion hurts India and Pakistan much more. There has been a huge 101 per cent increase in India's internal security (Home Ministry) budget in the last 5 years. For a more detailed analysis perhaps a part of India's defence budget should also be taken into account. But more importantly as policing

is a state subject, the hike in central government budget alone does not represent the full picture. We have no detailed study of how security expenditure has gone up in terrorism-affected states—Mahendra P. Lama, quoting from Paul Wallace, says that security budget in Punjab went up by 20 fold from Rs 150 million in early 1980s to more than 3 billion in 1992.[28] In Kashmir, for instance, apart from bearing the principal cost of peace keeping through the army and paramilitary forces, central government has been reimbursing all security-related expenditure (cost of raising reserve battalions, housing, transportation, medical expenses, etc.) —from 1989 to March 31, 2011, a Rs 3,583.30 crore has been transferred to the state government on this account.[29]

In case of central government spending the key elements are: increased spending on Central Para-Military Forces (CPMF), cost of building new institutions like NATGRID, NIA, NCTC and expansion of existing units like regional NSG hubs, providing funds for capacity building of state police forces and vastly enhanced cost of digital security.[30]

In terms of Pakistan, it is far more difficult to investigate the actual amount of diversion. There has been little change in terms of Pakistan's internal security budget but its defence budget has predictably gone up sharply during this period (post 2006) when the army launched its offensive against the militants in border areas.

Individuals and businesses in terror-affected areas are also made to pay the so-called terror tax (i.e. increase in transactional cost) in different ways. In terms of individuals, the chief cost is due to displacement—we have already mentioned massive internal displacement in Pakistan due to this so-called War on Terror. In India also, Kashmiri Pandit community represents a case for systematic targeting by terrorists resulting in displacement of the entire community from their original homeland that is Kashmir Valley. According to Home Ministry statistics, a total of 58,697 Kashmiri

Pandit families were forced to migrate out of the valley during the early part of the militancy. Most of these—38,119 families are living in the Jammu region, 19,338 families are living in New Delhi and the rest in other states/union territories. Jammu & Kashmir government, Delhi government and other state governments have been providing cash support to eligible families and large-scale housing projects have been taken up in different parts of Jammu to provide accommodation to them.[31]

For any business, there is a sharp hike in insurance premium if the establishment is located in a state/locality where security is a serious concern. Almost every business/office establishment in metropolitan India today is forced to invest considerable resources in securing their premises. Man Guarding constitutes +60 per cent followed by electronic security system at +25 per cent.[32] There are over 5,000 private security companies in operation and 5 million private security guards have been deployed for securing housing, industry business and community centres.[33] Smart entrepreneurs have cashed in this general sense of insecurity as private security business is one of the fastest growing businesses in India today. But it is important to underline that all these add to the cost of transacting business.

As business centres, tourist places, and citizens are becoming common targets, security today is a key concern to business, individuals, government. Indian security market was valued at around US$ 3 billion for 2010 and is estimated at a rate of 17 by 2015. India is estimated to be amongst the Top 10 security markets in the world by 2020.[34] Among the major spenders are airports, mass transport and maritime sectors. The size of the Indian electronic physical security (EPS) market was US$ 256 million in 2007 as per the report of the Security industry association. This market is expected to increase an average of 31 per cent a year from 2008 to 2012. In 2008, it is projected to grow to US$ 334 million, led by growth in CCTV and fire detection, the two largest product segments. Growth in these two technologies is being driven by rapid residential construction requiring fire detection and alarm equipment. CCTV is also driven by the rapidly expanding retail market.[35] Corporate organisations are estimated to have upped security budgets by 35-40 per cent during the recent years. [36]

The present situation poses different challenges for both the government as well as the private sector. Important private offices like the campus of software major Infosys in Bengaluru are now being protected by a specially trained Central Paramilitary force, CISF. Similarly, almost all the important temples around the country are being protected either by the central forces or an elite commando unit of the concerned state police. CISF is also deployed in Metro railways in Delhi and Kolkata just like airports. Important research institutions (following blast at Indian Institute of Science in Bengaluru) and even courts (after repeated targeting by terrorists) are being protected by gun-toting paramilitary forces. Elite NSG commandoes are deployed in every domestic flight. It is important at least for analytical purpose to see in detail how terrorism fuelled insecurity leads to massive cost burden on the economy at different levels.

It was mainly with the purpose of tracking terror financing that certain measures were introduced in Indian financial system. The foremost among those is the Know-Your-Customer, KYC norms in banking and financial institutions. Short-lived Cash Transaction Tax is also believed to have helped in this regard. One industry, which has suffered most due to security concerns, is telecom. A security transmutation is now taking place in Indian telecom sector after the telecom-terror nexus has been established. Indian government has just launched a nationwide voice and data monitoring project with an initial cost of Rs. 450 crore. This is the most comprehensive live monitoring possible at the moment of telecom traffic via wireless, terrestrial cables, sea cables and satellites modes. A number of monitoring nodes are in operation and more are in pipeline. Terror—mobile nexus has brought security at center stage of the telecom policies. Active use of mobiles in several terror blasts including infamous attack on Indian parliament in 2001 and attack on Mumbai have come up as a major security challenge for security forces. Open *Wi-Fi*, terror mails, unprotected cybercafes have forced authorities to look for a comprehensive framework on telecom security. A compulsory security identification of mobile subscriber has become a practice now. Government has also forced a ban on SMS service in J&K with a limited network at border areas.

India has barred import of mobile phones without identity code[37], followed by the ban/monitoring/security clearance of Chinese equipment import.[38] Terror threat has pushed authorities to broaden their horizon on telecom security and the office of National Security Adviser (under PMO) has become the center point for strategic coordination. MHA has dictated tough security stipulations for global push mail service providers like Blackberry (for putting a nodal server on Indian soil) and started ramping up decryption capacities at the level of security agencies. Cyber forensic institutions, top level intelligence agencies, telecom labs and experts have now been roped in to formulate a comprehensive Cyber security policy for India. This is the first time when manufacturing and import of telecom technologies/gears was also brought under the telecom security deliberations.

Real time monitoring of mobile calls is already in full swing.[39] Companies have been ordered to keep call data records for the longer duration. Compulsory security certification for import of telecom gears and technologies and security led guidelines for management of telecom companies have already been implemented. A National Telecom Security Policy and a New Telecom Manufacturing Policy are ready. A nationwide telecom-monitoring network, centralised cyber content monitoring system and a real time location via mobile phone are in the pipeline.

This serious concern for security has also aided certain long term changes in our economic behaviour to some extent. After repeated terror attacks at crowded markets like Sarojini Nagar, people feel more secured in hanging out or shopping inside a mall, where there are entry barriers, metal detectors and pat-down searches. This is no way to suggest that this change is solely due to security concerns but to a certain extent security has played a role here. Similarly, the issue of segregated and community-centric housing is an unfortunate fall out of security concerns[40].

Bomb and the Bill

Terrorism is normally seen as a political and law and order problem and as such responses are always designed from that perspective. Most observers do notice the asymmetric nature of warfare unleashed by terrorists, but till recently there was not much effort to understand the actual nature of damage caused by terrorism. Impact or economic consequences of a terror attack is never limited to direct cost alone. Total cost of terror is an aggregate of individual and government responses. Terror forces an individual to modify his/her investment and consumption patterns. Terror also forces a government to change its priorities, very often that means increasing security expenditure and curtailing equal amount of funding for socio-economic development. This is the actual cost that an act of terrorism imposes on any society. Beyond government finances, terrorism also leads to a serious distortion in terms of capital formation and growth in general. Certain industries are immediately affected, other industries may or may not be affected following an act of terror; but over a period of time any economy living under constant threat of insecurity suffer sub-optimal resource allocation. Targeting private or commercial properties in particular leads to fall in capital formation and thereby affects overall economic growth.

The way economic consequences of terrorism have been analysed in the West that may not be the right matrix for South Asia, which is a victim of long-term high intensity terrorism. But construction of a new paradigm would require in-depth field studies and adequate data, both of which are absent here. In terms of policy response, there is an urgent need to appreciate how exactly terrorism affects different levels of economy and formulate policy accordingly rather than simply increasing annual budget allocation for the affected state for every possible category.

Immediately after 9/11, the US launched three operations, ostensibly to make both the US and world a safer place—Operation Enduring Freedom in Afghanistan, Operation Iraqi Freedom and Operation Noble Eagle to make US military bases and homeland more secure. Out of these three, Operation Noble Eagle is the least known and Washington has spent least amount on it (total allocation in fact came down from US$ 8 billion in 2003 to US$ 100 million per annum beginning 2008),[41] yet it has been the most successful so far in terms of making the US more secure. Contribution of two other high-profile campaigns in making American life more secure—despite much higher cost—remain highly questionable. So the basic policy challenge for governments—more so in developing countries like India and Pakistan is to avoid the traps of asymmetric war, and allocate resources judiciously and effectively.

Notes

1. See Comptroller of the City of New York (2002), "One Year Later: the Fiscal Impact of 9/11 on New York City". http://comptroller.nyc.gov/bureaus/bud/reports/impact-9-11-year-later.pdf For a slightly different estimate, Gary Becker and Kevin Murphy "Prosperity Will Rise Out of the Ashes," *Wall Street Journal*, October 29, 2001. http://www.milkeninstitute.org/publications/publications.taf?function=detail&ID=102&cat=Arts. See also, Peter Navarro and Aron Spencer,

"September 11, 2001: Assessing the Costs of Terrorism," *The Milken Institute Review*, Fourth Quarter 2001. http://www.milkeninstitute.org/publications/review/2001_12/16-31mr.pdf

2. US Department of Transportation, *Treatment of the Economic Value of a Statistical Life in Departmental Analyses*, 2005. http://ostpxweb.dot.gov/policy/reports/080205.htm

3. Paul Krugman, *The Costs of Terrorism: What do we Know?* Briefing Note in a seminar at Princeton, 2004. http://www.l20.org/publications/9_7Q_wmd_krugman.pdf James R. Barth, Tong Li, Don McCarthy, Triphon Phumiwasana, and Glenn Yago, Economic Impacts of Global Terrorism: From Munich to Bali. Milken Institute, 2006. http://papers.ssrn.com/sol3/Delivery.cfm/SSRN_ID892033_code478764.pdf?abstractid=892033&mirid=1. This particular report gives details regarding various cost estimates of terror attacks. See also, Blomberg, S. Brock, Gregory D. Hess and Athanasios Orphanides. "The Macroeconomic Consequences of Terrorism," *Journal of Monetary Economics*, vol. 51(5), 2004, pp. 1007-1032; Blomberg, S. Brock, Gregory Hess and Akila Weerapana, "An Economic Model of Terrorism," *Conflict Management and Peace Science*, vol. 21, 2004, pp. 17-28; Walter Enders and Eric Olson, "Measuring the Economic Costs of Terrorism", Department of Economics Finance and Legal Studies, Culverhouse College of Commerce & Business Administration University of Alabama. http://www.socsci.uci.edu/~mrgarfin/OUP/papers/Enders.pdf

4. The only paper we have come across, which sought to address the issue in the context of India is Mahendra P Lama, "Terrorism and Insurgency in India: Economic Costs and Consequences", 2005. http://www.inflibnet.ac.in/ojs/index.php/JARPS/article/view/275/268 Written for CPA's project *Terrorism and the Rule of Law*, this article, although rich in data and anecdotes, does not really present a focused analysis of economic consequences of terrorism in India.

5. There are some works on economic cost of war in Sri Lanka, see for example, Nisha Arunatilake, Sisira Jayasuriya & Saman Kelegama, "The Economic Cost of the War in Sri Lanka", *World Development*, 29: 9, September 2001, pp. 1483-1500.

6. Jim Saxton (R-NJ), Chairman, Joint Economic Committee, United States Congress, *The Economic Costs of Terrorism*, May 2002. https://www.google.co.in/url?sa=t&rct=j&q=&esrc=s&source=web&cd=1&sqi=2&ved=0CDEQFjAA&url=http%3A%2F%2Fwww.hsdl.org%2F%3Fview%26did%3D3945&ei=KDzVUISZMMv9rAfb-ICYAQ&usg=AFQjCNHX8HKzYyu4bX47u1BhxdRpzBXY_Q

7. Ross Devol, Armen Bedroussian, Frank Fogelbach, Nathaniel Goetz, Ramon

Gonzalez, and Perry Wong, The Impact of September 11 on US Metropolitan Areas, Milken Institute Research Report, January 2002. http://www.milkeninstitute.org/pdf/National_Metro_Impact_Report.pdf
8. Jim Saxton, 2002.
9. Ibid.
10. Zvi Eckstein and Daniel Tsiddon, "Macroeconomic Consequences of Terror: Theory and the Case of Israel", Working Paper No. 7-2004, March 2004, the Foerder Institute for Economic Research and The Sackler Institute of Economic Studies. http://econ.tau.ac.il/papers/foerder/7-2004.pdf.
11. Two separate World Bank studies conclude that the cost of conflict on Israeli economy is about 4% of GDP and Palestinian economy on the other hand has suffered 50% declining from 1992 to 2003 due to this conflict.
12. Alberto Abadie, and J. Gardeazabal, "The Economic Costs of Conflict: A Case-Control Study for the Basque Country", *American Economic Review*, vol. 93(1), (2003), 113-132.
13. "The friction economy." *Fortune*, February 18, 2002,
14. Saxton, 2002; see also Smetters, Kent "Insuring Against Terrorism: The Policy Challenge", in Robert E. Lilan and Richard Herring, eds. *Brookings-Wharton Papers on Financial Services*. (2004), pp. 139-82.
15. http://www.start.umd.edu/gtd/. This database, originally started by Pinkerton Global Intelligence Services, is now being maintained by the University of Maryland with support from the Department of Homeland Security. This open source database has information regarding terrorism-related events from the 1970s to 2010.
16. Year wise no of attacks on rail network in India as per SATP database:
    1996 – 1
    1997 - 2
    1999 – 2
    2000 – 1
    2001 – 1
    2002 – 1
    2003 – 2
    2004 - 2
    2005 - 4
    2006 – 5
    2007 – 9
    2008 – 7
    2009 – 50
    2010 – 36
    2011 – 24

Most of these attacks have taken place in the North East and in Naxal-affected areas. It may also be mentioned that SATP has collected these data from limited number of newspapers.
17. http://www.finance.gov.pk/survey_1011.html
18. Alberto Abadie and Javier Gardeazabal.. "Terrorism and the World Economy," Working Paper, Harvard Kennedy School of Government, 2005, http://ksghome.harvard.edu/~aabadie/twe.pdf. Walter Enders and Todd Sandler. "Terrorism and Foreign Direct Investment in Spain and Greece," *Kyklos*, vol. 49(3), 1996, pp. 331-52. Volker Nitsch and Dieter Schumacher "Terrorism and International Trade: An Empirical Investigation," *European Journal of Political Economy*, vol. 20, 2004, pp. 423-433. Also see, William E James, "Indonesia's External Trade and Competitiveness: Assessing the Economic Costs of terrorism", paper presented at the USAID-CSIS Seminar on Economic Cost of Terrorism: Indonesia's responses", May 2002, Jakarta. http://pdf.usaid.gov/pdf_docs/PNACR189.pdf . Both Abadie and Gardeazabal and Enders and Sandler have found negative correlations between increasing number of terror attacks and declining foreign direct investment. Nitsch and Schumacher show how countries affected by terrorism trade less with each other – India and Pakistan ideally fit into this category.
19. Arshad Ali, *Economic Cost of Terrorism: A Case Study of Pakistan*. www.issi.org.pk/publication files/1299569657_66503137.pdf Pakistan Economic Survey 2010-11.
20. Since the beginning of the insurgency till the end of January 2011, 13,846 civilians and 4,807 security personnel have been killed in Kashmir, Home Ministry Annual Report 2011-12. Please see Table 3.
21. Amy Waldman, "Border Tension a Growth Industry for Kashmir", *New York Times*, October 18, 2002. http://www.arches.uga.edu/~sga/readings/kashmir_growth_industry.htm .
22. Details would be found in Annual Reports of the Union Home Ministry. For example in Nov, 2004 Prime Minister announced a special package of Rs 24,000 crore for the state. It may not be out of place to mention that the state of J&K has one of the lowest poverty ratios in the country and one of the highest percentages of population in government employment.
23. See Arshad Ali, op. cit.
24. It is an interesting coincidence how terrorism, in different time period, has destroyed tourism on both sides of the border – in two of the most picturesque destinations of India and Pakistan. A number of studies have looked at the comprehensive damage inflicted on tourism by terrorism. Some of the studies have also focused on how tourist inflow gets diverted due to one or a few

incidents and then take years to come back to the original destination. Milken Institute Report, 2006 gives the details.

25. Efraim Benmelech, Claude Berrebi and Esteban F. Klor: *The Economic Cost of Harbouring Terrorism*, Working Paper 15465, National Bureau of Economic Research, October 2009. http://www.nber.org/papers/w15465.
26. All data used in this paragraph so far is from SATP. http://www.satp.org/
27. Center for Research and Security Studies. http://crss.pk/beta/
28. Mahendra Lama, op. cit.
29. Home Ministry *Annual Report* 2011-2012.
30. Beginning with 2000-01, central government has been providing on an average Rs 1000 crore every year to the states for police modernization. Jammu & Kashmir and north-eastern states are eligible for 100% support under this scheme while other states get 75% reimbursement. Home Ministry Annual Report 2011-2012.
31. Govt of India decided to construct 5,242 two roomed tenements with an (initially projected) expenditure of Rs 385 crores to accommodate all the migrant families presently living in different camps in one roomed tenements in Jammu. In the 1st Phase, construction of 1,024 tenements at Nagrota, Purkhoo and Muthi have been completed and allotted. In the 2nd Phase, as on November 2011, out of 4,218, 3,654 have been completed and alloted. Rest are likely to be completed soon. Further, 200 flats are being constructed at Sheikhupora in Budgam district at a cost of Rs 22.90 crores - 180 of them already completed, rest of them are expected to be completed soon. Another 18 flats have also been constructed at Mattan. Annual Report 2011-12. Ministry of Home Affairs, Chapter II, pp. 14-16. Entire report available as PDF in the Ministry's website http://www.mha.nic.in
32. http://www.assocham.org/events/recent/event_574/mr.-rituraj-kishore-sinha-chief-operation-officer-coo-sis-india-ltd..pdf
33. http://www.slideshare.net/muthep/security-presentation-3373051
34. http://www.assocham.org/events/recent/event_574/mr.-rituraj-kishore-sinha-chief-operation-officer-coo-sis-india-ltd..pdf
35. http://www.siaonline.org/uploadedFiles/SIA/Research_and_Technology/SIA_International_Market_Reports/INDIA_SMR_Factsheet_0909_FINAL.pdf
36. http://www.slideshare.net/muthep/security-presentation-3373051
37. http://www.livemint.com/Companies/OKzS4Mm6yWt7yD86jR8qZN/Govt-bans-import-of-mobile-phones-sans-IMEI-number.html
38. http://www.ft.com/cms/s/0/6e5f923a-53b8-11df-aba0-00144feab49a.html
39. Based on govt. documents and discussion with security agencies.
40. Again, there are only anecdotal evidence but increasingly it is becoming a norm in our metro cities, particularly in New Delhi and Mumbai to restrict

access to housing. Despite being ready to pay the required price/rent, it is becoming difficult – and in certain pockets, impossible for Muslims to find accommodation. There are plenty of newspaper reports on the subject. See for instance a sensitive coverage in *The Hindu*, July 08, 2012, "Closing the door on Muslims in our cities".

41. Amy Belasco, *The Cost of Iraq, Afghanistan, and Other Global War on Terror Operations Since 9/11*, Congressional Research Service, March 2011.

9. Cinematic Interpretations of Terrorism-Images, Identity, and Impressions in Hindi Cinema

Swati Bakshi

I do not remember the first story book that I read in my childhood, but I would never fail to narrate the story of the first movie I had watched. This is not to suggest that I was disinterested in story books but the fact that the imprints of visual narratives are immensely strong. They create a space for themselves and refuse to fade till they are challenged by a new logic or knowledge. Visual narratives affect your brain and body in ways you may not be able to detect. Because most of the time they transmit ideas through emotions and not through intellect. That is why Cinema is considered as one of the most powerful medium of mass communication for its impact goes beyond the boundaries of time and place.

Theoretically speaking, there are two most popular theories on mass media that help us understand the effect of mass mediums: the Hypodermic theory and the selective perception theory. The hypodermic theory views mass culture as injections of propaganda or socialisation into a totally passive anaesthetised audience. It is sometimes argued that the function of the media is to anaesthetize the audience, the present day equivalent to the Marx's opiate of society. The selective perception theory believes that mass media plays the social function of reinforcing people's prejudices and pre-formed opinions rather than enlightening or correcting them.

The third approach, which developed as a reaction to such kind of pessimistic approaches towards media, is the cultural approach that highlights media as a major cultural and ideological force with respect to the ways in which socio-political issues are defined and popular ideologies are produced and transformed. It reflects on the selective construction social knowledge and cinema being one of the most powerful medium plays a vital role in disseminating this kind of selective knowledge.

We can understand the representation of terrorism in Hindi Cinema in this context. How certain identities have been produced and reproduced for that matter. Why only a certain kind of image appears on the screen again and again and why Cinema never goes beyond a certain point and hesitates in presenting a brave new world of ideas, incidents and explanations? Films circulate impressions of nations and nationalities and visual imageries associated with it and in a way condition human minds to accept it as the real knowledge. They give you an image of unknown or not so well known, which appears as true as reality in the absence of an encounter with reality.

Indian cinema has completed 100 years of its existence and obviously in these years things have drastically changed—new developments in political, economic and social sphere have been witnessed. Cinema being an important document of social history has more or less captured/reflected major moments of transformation in its own way.

Cinematic History –The Journey So far...
The most notable thing about Hindi Cinema is that we may analyze it in terms of Genre, style, content, representative qualities, time and space but its basic identity remains tied with song and dance or what we call *Masala* films.

But one cannot disagree with the fact that Hindi popular cinema is a curious mix of serious real-life issues generously laced with song and dance and other elements of mass entertainment. These different elements in right proportions have ensured super success of many films and with some variations it still continues. However in the context of world cinema Indian mainstream is a genre of its own—entertainment gets priority here most of the time but ever so often it manages to hit the right note in terms of changing social-economic and psychological context.

The Golden 50s

The decades of 1950s and 60s are referred to as the golden era of Hindi Cinema. This period is remembered for immense creativity, originality, and unmatched talent that emerged in Cinema. A variety of factors influenced film making during this era such as the Indian People's Theatre Group, India's first International film festival (IFFI), painful process of Partition and its memories, Nation-building process in Post Independence era, issues of socio-economic development, large scale rural to urban migration.

The city became a new found place for growth and employment, dreams and desires but also a site of disparities, exploitations and crime. That is why we have a large number of patriotic films in the wake of newly found Independence on the one hand and genre of crime thrillers like on the other.

The New Wave

The decade of 1960 also witnessed the rise and growth of what we call art house cinema or new wave of Hindi cinema, even though the wave started not from Mumbai but from Bengal. Filmmaker Satyajit Ray's *Pather Panchali* (1955) was not just a film, it triggered a wave that changed the destiny of Cinema in India itself. Ritwik Ghatak, Mrinal Sen, and Satyajit Ray began making films within a few years of each other, and set the stage right for the emergence of New Wave, which flourished with filmmakers like Basu Chatterji, Mani

Kaul, Govind Nihalani, Saeed Akhtar Mirza and Shyam Benegal. Film Finance Corporation and Film Institute at Mumbai (now FTII) played a major role in this era.

An era of crisis and rise of Angry Young Man- 1970's and 80's
The hope filled journey of Independent India received major setbacks in 1970's when hope for a better life began to diminish. War with Pakistan, the burden of refugee relief, acute droughts in 1971 and 1972, food shortage, spiralling inflation and unemployment lead to political unrest. The country witnessed widespread demonstrations, street protests, and violent disruptions. This decade saw the severest political crisis of India's democratic history—the emergency imposed by the then PM Indira Gandhi in 1975. Twenty-one months of emergency was a period of freaking censorship and unrest.

Director Prakash Mehra's *Zanjeer* (1973) was released against this background which heralded the era of angry young man portrayed by Amitabh Bachchan films after film. This angry young man was violent, cynical urban worker or labourer whose anger was against either unjust corrupt system or exploitation of disadvantaged sections by wealthy people.

In the chaotic period of 70s and 80s the time was apt for this type of hero to emerge who is fearless and who fights for his dignity as people could relate with this anger and distrust. Thus, the kind of figures appear on screen are reflections of social realities of the time. This fact gives them wider acceptance, success and impact

Liberalisation, Globalisation, and Global Bollywood—the 1990s
Hindi cinema has always reflected the socio-political realities of a particular time. But there is certainly something extra ordinary about the 1990s. This particular decade witnessed some of the most significant developments in the social, political and economic life of India.

In 1991, Indian Government initiates economic reforms to liberalize economy and with that enters globalization and its implications for a society marked by several complexities. The decade of the 1990s is also crucial in terms of various political developments. Insurgency reached to its peak in Kashmir. This was also the era of rising Hindu Nationalism, which reached its crescendo with Babri Masjid demolition and sectarian violence. Between 1995 to 2005, Nuclear tests and border conflict in Kargil which is described as Kargil war—all these factors impacted the Cinema both in terms of theme and feel.

The kind of films that began to appear in this period was completely different from the rest of the cinematic history of India. Liberal economic policies opened doors to the opportunities available worldwide, access to international dreams was made possible in this liberal and global world. Since 1991, state economic policies have catered mainly to the ambitious urban middle class consumer who can be attracted towards automobiles, cosmetics and household appliances and carbonated drinks.

In this consumer-driven globalised world, *Dilwale Dulhaniya Le Jayenge*(1995) arrived and wrote a new history of cinematic success. In terms of look, feel and theme, *DDLJ* changed the subsequent course of Hindi Cinema. The NRI who was used in Hindi films for comic relief, as a human being with lost values returns in *DDLJ*'s Raj Malhotra (Shahrukh Khan) as *pakka* Hindustani who may fail in university examinations but comes out with flying colours in his test of morality and values. The film conveys the message that, you don't need to be in India to be a true Indian. This is the return of the Nation in a new avatar.

It is not, however, that Nation had gone out of the films, never. In Hindi Cinema, the Nation was always located in a family where the central conflict rises, reaches to its peak and moves towards a climax. This nation despite not having gone anywhere returns with a vengeance in post-globalised Hindi Cinema.

In an economically liberalised India, Bollywood quickly understood the importance of the NRI. Rural, poverty stricken, unemployed *Bharat* suddenly disappeared in the global Bollywood. With liberalisation and globalisation the world came closer; foreign dreams and locations became easy to sell leaving no space for poor protagonists to appear on silver screen with stark realities of their lives.

The Politics of Identity in Bollywood films
On thematic level, as I have mentioned, the sentiment of Nationalism found its place in many films but with a difference. Now it was no longer the West which was seen as threat to native culture. The dichotomy was no longer between the East and the West' the definitive villain now is the Terrorist who threatens the very existence of the nation. Through the survey of few representative films, I want to establish three basic points here:
1. Resurgent nationalism in films based on the theme of Terrorism
2. The explicit naming of and focus on Pakistan as a source of terrorism with a simultaneous focus on Indian state as oppressive and inefficient in eradicating the root cause.
3. A search for global Muslim identity—post 9/11

This paper tries to capture how Hindi cinema has dealt with the issue of terrorism in sheer political terms and refrained from exploring complexities and effects in a society, in some of the commercially successful films. These films have been chosen on the basis of their representative qualities as far as depiction of terrorism in commercial Hindi Cinema is concerned.

Through these films, the purpose is to capture a forward movement in the ways how commercial Hindi cinema understands terrorism and realities that surfaced in all these decades. For instance we can discuss a whole lot of films from Border to *Maa*

Tujhe Salaam, Veer Zara or for that matter *Main Hoon Na* as they represent different perspectives on Indo-Pak relations and violence but this paper focuses on the treatment of the issue of terrorism in terms of changing global scenario along with a shift in Pakistan-centric discourse.

These films showcase how cinematic space has been used and approach towards understanding the reasons, structure and effects of the ideology of terrorism has changed.

There are many films in the realm which can be discussed about their treatment of the matter but my purpose here is to track the changing pattern of depiction of the issue and its repercussions in a dynamic world.

The first important film in this regard is *'Roja'*, director Mani Ratnam's first film of his trilogy on terrorism, released in 1992. This is also interesting to note that the Hindi Cinema (which is the same as Indian Cinema for most of the people) didn't come out with the idea of exploring the issue of terrorism. *Roja* which is referred to as the first Hindi film to talk about the issue of terrorism, came from the southern Indian filmmaker, Mani Ratnam who dubbed the film in Hindi to reach out to the wider audience.

Arvind Swamy plays Rishi Kumar, a cryptologist who works for Indian government. He gets married to a Tamil village girl Roja under strange circumstances when Roja's sister asks him to say no to their marriage as she is in love with someone else. Immediately after marriage, Rishi has to go to Kashmir on an assignment accompanied by Roja. There Rishi is abducted by the Kashmiri Jihadis and the story revolves around Roja's struggle to get her husband back.

Roja is a climactic film for it brings the two sides together the Indian state represented by Rishi Kumar and the jihadis. The film represents the ideological conflict between the nationalist victim and the jihadis. But if you look at the dialogues given to the characters you can clearly understand the ideological supremacy of the Indian state that prevails throughout the film.

Roja doesn't clearly name Pakistan as a breeding ground of terrorism but makes references like *bagal wale desh, sarhad paar,* etc. The film while dealing with the ideology and conflict never goes beyond the nationalistic agenda. *Roja* actually tries to explore the patriotic possibilities of terrorism in Kashmir. The director initiates a dialogue but takes it to a very predictable path where ultimately the Indian nation and love for this nation has to supersede.

There is a scene in the film where Pankaj Kapur as Liaquat—the jihadi, speaks to Rishi kumar.

Rishi kumar—क्यों कर रहे हो ये सब (why are you doing all this)

Liaquat- आज़ादी के लिए और इसके लिए हम कुछ भी कर सकते हैं
(to get freedom and we can go to any extent to achieve the same)
Rishi kumar- ये तुम्हारा भाई है ज़रूरत पड़ेगी तो मार दोगे इसे ?
(this is your brother if needed, will you kill him?)

Liaquat -- हां मार दूंगा (yes I will kill him)

Rishi kumar--तुम्हारी मां (your mother?)

Liaquat -- मार दूंगा (I will kill her)

Rishi kumar--तुम्हारी बहन (your sister?)

Liaquat --मार दूंगा (I will kill her)

These dialogues do not appear strange to the audience because they conform to the image of a jihadi as it has been projected—a fanatic, brutal being. Did you ever think why his side of story never comes on screen, his logic is never advocated? The reason is that the whole agenda of making a film is to establish a particular line of thought and in this case, the nation has to emerge as logical, benevolent and humane vis-a-vis a jihadi. So right from dialogues to music, every aspect works in the direction of stimulating the phenomenon of nationalism.

The end of the film is purely compromised to meet the requirements of an Indian nationalistic film where the protagonist who is a symbol of Indian nation state cannot be defeated or shown dead, otherwise you do not find a reason why he should not be killed by the extremists.

So, in *Roja* also, no introspection, no internal scrutiny of reasons leading to the current situation is signalled, and the audience returns with one memory: *bharat humko jaan se pyara hai* with Arvind Swamy protecting the tri-colour by risking his life against fire.

Maniratnam's next film in the series is *'Bombay' (1995)*. *Bombay* is said to be a water-shed movie because it came at a time of great tensions. The story unfolds in the backdrop of 1993 Mumbai blasts and the theme of inter religious marriage here becomes a strong message of communal harmony. The leading lady of the film who happens to be a Muslim elopes with a Hindu guy. They live together as a happy family until communal tensions broke out in Bombay in the aftermath of Babri Masjid demolition. Thus, it places the responsibility of terrorism on reactionary violence.

This film doesn't deal with cross border terrorism but with internal conflicts and explores the human cost of violence. This film also ends on a positive note but after posing many questions regarding society, religion and places an individual in the turbulent conditions to show how shallow are these concepts before love. It strongly recommends that love and humanity has no religion. So no hardcore political questions and answers are dealt with but the film calls for a more humane understanding of the problem of terrorism.

Maniratnam's triology on Terrorism concluded with *'Dil Se' (1998)*, once again dealing with the human side of terrorism. Maniratnam tried to explore the possibilities of love in the heart of a hard core terrorist played by Manisha Koirala but ultimately establishes the inclusive and sacrificing nature of the Indian state represented by the character played by Shahrukh Khan as an All India Radio employee.

However, a clear inkling of change appears on the Hindi silvescreen with Gulzar's *'Maachis' (1996)*. Gulzar who himself is filled with the memories of partition and riots that followed takes up the issue of militancy in Punjab during the 80s. *Maachis* is set in the turbulent Punjab of 1980s. It is a tale of youngsters being pushed into terrorism. The story takes off on Kirpal's (Chandrachur Singh) anguish over the detention and torture of his dear friend Jassi (Zutshi) on the suspicion of his links with the assassination of a politician in Delhi. A bitter and angry Kirpal who is also the fiancee of Jassi's sister Veeran (Tabu) meets a gang of militants through his bus journey. These militants are from across the border and other youths who, like him, have been victims of police high-handedness and tragic events in Punjab.

What makes *Maachis* important is that for the first time we see a film which places the responsibility of making terrorists on the unjust, corrupt and oppressive state, which forces young people to resort to violence when their voices go unheard.

Thus, *Maachis* tries to engage in a dialogue and establishes that a terrorist is not a terrorist by birth; society is responsible to a great extent and hints at the need for mending the system that forces people to resort to weapons. Thus Gulzar calls for introspection here.

The character of Sanatan played by Om Puri, who becomes a terrorist after his whole family was killed in anti-sikh riots explains to Kirpal:

Kirpal—तुम्हारी पार्टी का नाम क्या है (what is the name of your party?)

Sanatan- मेरी कोई पार्टी नहीं है. ना ही मैं किसी धर्म की लड़ाई लड़ रहा हूं. मैं तो अपनी बेबसी की लड़ाई लड़ रहा हूं. ये सिस्टम मुझे नामर्द साबित करना चाहता है लेकिन मैं नामर्द नहीं हूं. (I don't have a party. Neither am I fighting for any religion. This fight comes out of my helplessness. This system intends to prove me as impotent but I am not.)

At another place he is shown expressing his anger in words like ये मुल्क self sufficient नहीं हुआ कुछ लोग self sufficient ज़रूर हो गए है. बिजली,पानी,दवाई...कौन सी चीज़ है जो आम आदमी को नसीब हो गई है.

(This country hasn't become self sufficient; only a few people have become self sufficient. Medicine, water, electricity tell me which basic need of a common man has been fulfilled.)

So Gulzar, in my view, has gone a step further in exploring the psyche of a terrorist rather than dismissing him as a fanatic. But another important factor and the common one that goes with *Maachis* also is the reference of Pakistan and its role in promoting militancy and instability in India.

In a scene, Sanatan explains to the group that they have to wait for a rocket shooter (Tabu) who has been trained across the border. So the director has a clear cut impression that Pakistan is the grooming ground of terrorism, which he conveniently projects though he chooses not to take the name. Gulzar acknowledges the role of Pakistan in training and arming militants but he never defocuses from the narrative that asserts that internal conflicts are responsible for secessionist tendencies and the state needs to look into its own system and agencies as well. So, here is a film that dares to call for self assessment and resolution of internal discontents.

From 1999 onwards, we have a complete shift in the political culture of Hindi cinema. You can clearly notice the bhagwa nationalism colouring the cinematic vision, opening a floodgate for super nationalistic films where the tone and texture of cinema confirms to the popular sentiment and at the same time to the dominant political ideology. Post-Kargil emotions were clear. India had recently conducted nuclear tests so the sense of power and protection of nationhood figure prominently on silver screen. There is an increasing focus on Pakistan as a major source of terrorism. The film makers do not find the need to go beyond this belief and search for more dimensions or explain the complexities involved.

Let's begin the survey of this phase with *'Sarfarosh' (1999)* where Aamir Khan plays ACP Rathod. *Sarfarosh* goes many steps further in overtly identifying Pakistan as a source of instability, both on maps used in the narrative and in dialogues but it also weaves a number of real life events—the links between Mumbai underworld dons and Pakistan's intelligence agency ISI, weapon smuggling and so on.

The film tries to construct a complex tale of art, law-enforcement and international crime. *Sarfarosh* is significant because it also tries to capture the Muslim minority and its sentiments through the marginalised figure of Inspector Salim played by actor Mukesh Rishi. Police establishment is doubtful about his honesty in arresting Muslim criminals, while his own community mocks at his allegiance to the police which persecutes followers of Islam. So it tries to establish the impression that being a Muslim your loyalties are somewhat under scanner but the purpose isn't to go any further on this.

The film through this character also seeks to establish the nationalistic discourse as Naseeruddin Shah who plays Gulfam Hassan and who is a Muhajir in Pakistan is at last abandoned by ISI while Salim is apologised to by Rathod. The implicit message is that Indian Muslims still have possibilities of acceptance, unlike ethnic minority Muslims in Pakistan. In other words it seeks to establish that Pakistan still suffers from the insecurities of Partition while India has moved on. Muslims who willingly stayed here have every chance of being treated as equal citizens while the Muslims who migrated to Pakistan still lead the life of a refugee called as Muhajir (as Gulfam

Hassan is repeatedly described by Pakistani operatives). Even if they show their loyalties to the Pakistani Nation, they aren't treated well and are seen with hatred and distrust.

The year 2000 marks yet another shift in the Pakistan-centric discourse in Hindi cinema with the release of *'Mission Kashmir'* and *'Fiza'* within months of each other. Both films starred Hrithik Roshan. While *Fiza* presents Muslim marginalisation and militarisation as being a result of the rise of Hindu nationalism (in specific pinning the blames on the Mumbai riots of 1993 following the Babri Masjid demolition), *Mission Kashmir* is a more complex tale. It takes place in the backdrop of militancy in Kashmir in the 1990s, and depicts how a state oppression leads a young orphan to militancy.

The film as most of the Hindi films does, locates the conflict within the family as a symbol of the Indian nation. An Ideal Kashmiri family with a Hindu wife and a Muslim husband, Inayat Khan, played by Sanjay Dutt, who is a police officer responsible for the security of Kashmir.

As the story unfolds, Inayat Khan kills a band of extremists and along with them a Muslim family (with whom the terrorists had taken shelter) while the sole survivor of the family, 9-year old Altaf watches the masked Khan destroying his entire family. Wife Nilima (Sonali Kulkarni) persuades Khan to bring home the boy, especially since the duo recently lost their only son in an accident. A little later the boy, Altaf, realises that the man he has come to call his 'abba' is in fact the man who torments him in his nightmares, and flees to become a terrorist (Hrithik Roshan). Altaf swears vengeance against Khan, and instigated by the Afghani terrorist Hilal Kohistani (Jackie Shroff) who conceives of Mission Kashmir to disintegrate India, he almost succeeds in this. Till, of course, love wins over hatred or, Kashmiriyat over Azaadi.

The family, and thereby, the nation is shown traumatised by the extremist violence and the reciprocal violence throughout the film. The film tried to establish that Muslim families give shelter to terrorists; therefore they themselves become the victim, an attempt to say that the state is bound to act. However, Mission Kashmir again ends on a forced reconciliation where the state once again shows its liberal nature and embraces a terrorist whose lost sense of judgement seems to be restored. So, even when Director Vidhu Vinod Chopra attempts at taking up the issue of State sponsored violence and its reactionary effect, he fails to take it into the realm of unspoken and unseen realities.

Mission Kashmir is noteworthy in a sense that it gradually shifts the focus from Pakistan-centric source of instability to globalised terror networks as the film includes a shadowy figure distinctly reminiscent of Osama bin Laden, the puppet master or the overlord whose loyalties are with no single nation, a non state actor and the western neighbour is shown as a small fish in the larger geo-strategic game. So here you have a film which tries to locate terrorism in a global world and moves beyond Pakistan fixation.

Director Khalid Mohammed, on the other hand, ends *Fiza* on a tragic note with the death of the protagonists. He possibly couldn't find a solution for the Muslim minority in India. The film is a complex articulation of Indian Muslim's fear regarding its minority status, which prompts them to take up weapons to protect themselves. Towards the climax, Fiza the sister kills her brother so that he doesn't fall into the hands of the police; thus, maintaining the distrust, insecurity and unresolved hatred and questioning the role of the state towards its citizen.

Another major change in the realm of representation of terrorism comes post-9/11 Attacks on twin towers, the US war on terror and its implications for Asians have completely changed the paradigm of Hindi cinema as far as dealing with terrorism is concerned. The focus is not on internal turmoil and oppression anymore but on the misunderstanding about Islam and a search of global identity for Muslims. Films like *'New York'*, *'My Name Is Khan'*, *'A Wednesday'*, etc. deal with the Muslim insecurities in a globalised world.

The most striking thing about the film *'New York' (2009)* is the placing of Muslim characters in a global context—well educated global citizens. Their identity is not through their religion here as they are not given any religion specific elements. They are comfortably integrated global citizens rather than nostalgic NRI's of post-globalisation era. But things suddenly change for them as they become the victims of 9/11 attacks. Their religious identity becomes the root cause of suspicion, hatred and destruction as the world around them becomes Islamophobic.

The film is significant in the sense that it highlights many themes- the atrocities carried out by the American intelligence, how terrorists can be created, issues of human rights violation, insecurities of a Muslim in a liberal and globalised world. The film poses many questions—who is to be blamed, who is the victim, aren't the Muslims victim themselves.

It also brings out the issues of human rights violation especially against the Asians in America post 9/11. *New York* also marks the gradual shift of Pakistan centric discourse to a non-Pakistan centric and a more self-reflexive kind of cinema.

Another film that took this trend to another level is *'My Name Is Khan'* (2010). Shahrukh Khan's dialogue as Rizwan Khan in the film 'My name is Khan' and 'I am not a terrorist' speaks for the Muslims of the world, their insecurities, their dilemma. Rizwan says his prayers in public, wears his cap, derives his identity from his religion, but rises well above it and thus this character holds a mirror to the world. *My Name Is Khan* depicts a strong desire and urgency on the part of the Muslims to erase misunderstandings about Islam and its message, across the globe. So, it is a search of an identity in the world without borders and this search would end only when the world realizes in the form of a US President in the film who declares before the world that 'his name is khan and he is not a terrorist'.

However, a recent film by Neeraj Pandey gave a new dimension to the way films have dealt with the issue of terrorism on screen. Till now, it was state vs terrorists. *'A Wednesday' (2008)* by debutant Neeraj brings the 'stupid common man' on silver screen, who wants to get rid of terrorists in this country. This common man is not recognised by his religious identity but the terrorists that he wants to kill are all Muslims. This film knowingly or unknowingly validates reactionary violence. It is the same logic by which a Samjhauta express explosion or malegaon blasts can be validated.

The common man played by Naseeruddin Shah asks

अगर आपके घर में कॉक्रोच घुस आए तो आप क्या करते है.उसे मारते हैं ना. ये आतंकवादी मेरे देश में घुसकर उसे गंदा कर रहे थे. मैंने इन्हें मारकर अपने देश को साफ़ किया है.

(What do you do when you see a cockroach in your house? You kill it. These terrorists were smudging my land. I have killed them to clean up my country.)

So the phenomenon of aggressive Nationalism once again grips the silverscreen, but this time of the vigilante sort. Here once again I would like to go back to the points that I made while starting off with this survey of films. In the last three decades, an increasing number of films have tended to deliberate on the phenomenon of resurgent nationalism in films based on the theme of Terrorism. These tend to resort to explicit naming of, and focus on, Pakistan as a source of terrorism with a simultaneous focus on Indian state as oppressive and inefficient in eradicating the root cause. Lately, a search for global Muslim identity has become discernible in the wake of 9/11.

So, right from *'Roja'* to *'A Wednesday'*, nationalism finds its place redefined in terms of opposition to terrorism. The terrorist becomes the tool of confirming superiority of the nation and you crave for something unusual and path breaking that never comes out in these films.

Undoubtedly, there is a shift from Pakistan-centric and partition-based construction of identities as films began to talk about hi-tech global terror networks using modern technology for the purpose of carrying out terror attacks but it never tries to go deep down and bring out the realities of everyday life in a terror stricken society, the human cost of terrorism is far more than we can imagine.

Films like *My Name Is Khan* and *New York* attempt to bring out post 9/11 insecurities of the Muslims across the world but the point here is that while dealing with the issue of terrorism Hindi cinema never moves beyond political ideologies and conflicts. We all carry the image of a terrorist in our minds even if we have never come across one in our lives, thanks to the films of course. It is perhaps time to deliberate on the question how generations brought up with such images would build their ideas about life and the outside world, and what impressions do they carry about human nature and humanity.

Select Bibliography
1. Fareed Kazmi, *The Politics of India's Conventional Cinema: Imaging a Universe, Subverting a Multiverse* (New Delhi: Sage Publishers, 1999).
2. Anirudh Deshpande, *Class Power and Consciousness in Indian Cinema and Television*, (New Delhi: Primus, 2009).
3. Kalyani Chaddha and Anandam V Kavoori, "Exoticized, Marginalised, Demonized: the Muslim 'Other' in Hindi Cinema", in Anandam Kavoori and Ashwin Punathambekar (eds) *Global Bollywood*, (New York: New York University Press, 2009).
4. Meenakshi Bharat and Nirmal Kumar (eds), *Filming the Line Of Control: the Indo-Pak Relationship through the Cinematic Lens*, (New Delhi: Routledge, 2007).
5. Ravi S. Vasudevan (ed), *Making Meaning of Indian Cinema*, (New Delhi: Oxford University Press, 2000).
6. Jabrimall Parikh, *Sanjha Sangharsh, Sampradyik Aatankwad aur Hindi Cinema*, (New Delhi: Shri Vani Prakashan, 2011).
7. Tejaswini Ganti, *Bollywood: A Guide to Popular Hindi Cinema*, (New Delhi: Routledge, 2004).